Visionary Secrets
of
AI Driverless Cars

Practical Advances in
Artificial Intelligence and Machine Learning

Dr. Lance B. Eliot, MBA, PhD

Disclaimer: This book is presented solely for educational and entertainment purposes. The author and publisher are not offering it as legal, accounting, or other professional services advice. The author and publisher make no representations or warranties of any kind and assume no liabilities of any kind with respect to the accuracy or completeness of the contents and specifically disclaim any implied warranties of merchantability or fitness of use for a particular purpose. Neither the author nor the publisher shall be held liable or responsible to any person or entity with respect to any loss or incidental or consequential damages caused, or alleged to have been caused, directly or indirectly, by the information or programs contained herein. Every company is different and the advice and strategies contained herein may not be suitable for your situation.

DEDICATION

To my incredible daughter, Lauren, and my incredible son, Michael.
Forest fortuna adiuvat (from the Latin; good fortune favors the brave).

CONTENTS

Lance B. Eliot

ACKNOWLEDGMENTS

I have been the beneficiary of advice and counsel by many friends, colleagues, family, investors, and many others. I want to thank everyone that has aided me throughout my career. I write from the heart and the head, having experienced first-hand what it means to have others around you that support you during the good times and the tough times.

To Warren Bennis, one of my doctoral advisors and ultimately a colleague, I offer my deepest thanks and appreciation, especially for his calm and insightful wisdom and support.

To Mark Stevens and his generous efforts toward funding and supporting the USC Stevens Center for Innovation.

To Lloyd Greif and the USC Lloyd Greif Center for Entrepreneurial Studies for their ongoing encouragement of founders and entrepreneurs.

To Peter Drucker, William Wang, Aaron Levie, Peter Kim, Jon Kraft, Cindy Crawford, Jenny Ming, Steve Milligan, Chis Underwood, Frank Gehry, Buzz Aldrin, Steve Forbes, Bill Thompson, Dave Dillon, Alan Fuerstman, Larry Ellison, Jim Sinegal, John Sperling, Mark Stevenson, Anand Nallathambi, Thomas Barrack, Jr., and many other innovators and leaders that I have met and gained mightily from doing so.

Thanks to Ed Trainor, Kevin Anderson, James Hickey, Wendell Jones, Ken Harris, DuWayne Peterson, Mike Brown, Jim Thornton, Abhi Beniwal, Al Biland, John Nomura, Eliot Weinman, John Desmond, and many others for their unwavering support during my career.

And most of all thanks as always to Michael and Lauren, for their ongoing support and for having seen me writing and heard much of this material during the many months involved in writing it. To their patience and willingness to listen.

INTRODUCTION

This is a book that provides the newest innovations and the latest Artificial Intelligence (AI) advances about the emerging nature of AI-based autonomous self-driving driverless cars. Via recent advances in Artificial Intelligence (AI) and Machine Learning (ML), we are nearing the day when vehicles can control themselves and will not require and nor rely upon human intervention to perform their driving tasks (or, that <u>allow</u> for human intervention, but only *require* human intervention in very limited ways).

Similar to my other related books, which I describe in a moment and list the chapters in the Appendix A of this book, I am particularly focused on those advances that pertain to self-driving cars. The phrase "autonomous vehicles" is often used to refer to any kind of vehicle, whether it is ground-based or in the air or sea, and whether it is a cargo hauling trailer truck or a conventional passenger car. Though the aspects described in this book are certainly applicable to all kinds of autonomous vehicles, I am focused more so here on cars.

Indeed, I am especially known for my role in aiding the advancement of self-driving cars, serving currently as the Executive Director of the Cybernetic Self-Driving Cars Institute.. In addition to writing software, designing and developing systems and software for self-driving cars, I also speak and write quite a bit about the topic. This book is a collection of some of my more advanced essays. For those of you that might have seen my essays posted elsewhere, I have updated them and integrated them into this book as one handy cohesive package.

You might be interested in companion books that I have written that provide additional key innovations and fundamentals about self-driving cars. Those books are entitled **"Introduction to Driverless Self-Driving Cars," "Advances in AI and Autonomous Vehicles: Cybernetic Self-Driving Cars," "Self-Driving Cars: "The Mother of All AI Projects," "Innovation and Thought Leadership on Self-Driving Driverless Cars," "New Advances in AI Autonomous Driverless Self-Driving Cars,"** and **"Autonomous Vehicle Driverless Self-Driving Cars and**

Artificial Intelligence," "Transformative Artificial Intelligence Driverless Self-Driving Cars," "Disruptive Artificial Intelligence and Driverless Self-Driving Cars, and "State-of-the-Art AI Driverless Self-Driving Cars," and "Top Trends in AI Self-Driving Cars," and "AI Innovations and Self-Driving Cars," "Crucial Advances for AI Driverless Cars," "Sociotechnical Insights and AI Driverless Cars," "Pioneering Advances for AI Driverless Cars" and "Leading Edge Trends for AI Driverless Cars," "The Cutting Edge of AI Autonomous Cars" and "The Next Wave of AI Self-Driving Cars" and "Revolutionary Innovations of AI Self-Driving Cars," and "AI Self-Driving Cars Breakthroughs," "Trailblazing Trends for AI Self-Driving Cars," "Ingenious Strides for AI Driverless Cars," "AI Self-Driving Cars Inventiveness," and "Visionary Secrets of AI Driverless Cars" (they are all available via Amazon). See Appendix A of this herein book to see a listing of the chapters covered in those three books.

For the introduction here to this book, I am going to borrow my introduction from those companion books, since it does a good job of laying out the landscape of self-driving cars and my overall viewpoints on the topic. The remainder of the book is all new material that does not appear in the companion books.

INTRODUCTION TO SELF-DRIVING CARS

This is a book about self-driving cars. Someday in the future, we'll all have self-driving cars and this book will perhaps seem antiquated, but right now, we are at the forefront of the self-driving car wave. Daily news bombards us with flashes of new announcements by one car maker or another and leaves the impression that within the next few weeks or maybe months that the self-driving car will be here. A casual non-technical reader would assume from these news flashes that in fact we must be on the cusp of a true self-driving car.

Here's a real news flash: We are still quite a distance from having a true self-driving car. It is years to go before we get there.

Why is that? Because a true self-driving car is akin to a moonshot. In the same manner that getting us to the moon was an incredible feat, likewise is achieving a true self-driving car. Anybody that suggests or even brashly states that the true self-driving car is nearly here should be viewed with great skepticism. Indeed, you'll see that I often tend to use the word "hogwash" or "crock" when I assess much of the decidedly *fake news* about self-driving cars. Those of us on the inside know that what is often reported to the outside is malarkey. Few of the insiders are willing to say so. I have no such hesitation.

Indeed, I've been writing a popular blog post about self-driving cars and hitting hard on those that try to wave their hands and pretend that we are on the imminent verge of true self-driving cars. For many years, I've been known as the AI Insider. Besides writing about AI, I also develop AI software. I do what I describe. It also gives me insights into what others that are doing AI are really doing versus what it is said they are doing.

Many faithful readers had asked me to pull together my insightful short essays and put them into another book, which you are now holding.

For those of you that have been reading my essays over the years, this collection not only puts them together into one handy package, I also updated the essays and added new material. For those of you that are new to the topic of self-driving cars and AI, I hope you find these essays approachable and informative. I also tend to have a writing style with a bit of a voice, and so you'll see that I am times have a wry sense of humor and poke at conformity.

As a former professor and founder of an AI research lab, I for many years wrote in the formal language of academic writing. I published in referred journals and served as an editor for several AI journals. This writing here is not of the nature, and I have adopted a different and more informal style for these essays. That being said, I also do mention from time-to-time more rigorous material on AI and encourage you all to dig into those deeper and more formal materials if so interested.

I am also an AI practitioner. This means that I write AI software for a living. Currently, I head-up the Cybernetics Self-Driving Car Institute, where we are developing AI software for self-driving cars. I am excited to also report that my son, also a software engineer, heads-up our Cybernetics Self-Driving Car Lab. What I have helped to start, and for which he is an integral part, ultimately he will carry long into the future after I have retired. My daughter, a marketing whiz, also is integral to our efforts as head of our Marketing group. She too will carry forward the legacy now being formulated.

For those of you that are reading this book and have a penchant for writing code, you might consider taking a look at the open source code available for self-driving cars. This is a handy place to start learning how to develop AI for self-driving cars. There are also many new educational courses spring forth. There is a growing body of those wanting to learn about and develop self-driving cars, and a growing body of colleges, labs, and other avenues by which you can learn about self-driving cars.

This book will provide a foundation of aspects that I think will get you ready for those kinds of more advanced training opportunities. If you've already taken those classes, you'll likely find these essays especially interesting as they offer a perspective that I am betting few other instructors or faculty offered to you. These are challenging essays that ask you to think beyond the conventional about self-driving cars.

THE MOTHER OF ALL AI PROJECTS

In June 2017, Apple CEO Tim Cook came out and finally admitted that Apple has been working on a self-driving car. As you'll see in my essays, Apple was enmeshed in secrecy about their self-driving car efforts. We have only been able to read the tea leaves and guess at what Apple has been up to. The notion of an iCar has been floating for quite a while, and self-driving engineers and researchers have been signing tight-lipped Non-Disclosure Agreements (NDA's) to work on projects at Apple that were as shrouded in mystery as any military invasion plans might be.

Tim Cook said something that many others in the Artificial Intelligence (AI) field have been saying, namely, the creation of a self-driving car has got to be the mother of all AI projects. In other words, it is in fact a tremendous moonshot for AI. If a self-driving car can be crafted and the AI works as we hope, it means that we have made incredible strides with AI and that therefore it opens many other worlds of potential breakthrough accomplishments that AI can solve.

Is this hyperbole? Am I just trying to make AI seem like a miracle worker and so provide self-aggrandizing statements for those of us writing the AI software for self-driving cars? No, it is not hyperbole. Developing a true self-driving car is really, really, really hard to do. Let me take a moment to explain why. As a side note, I realize that the Apple CEO is known for at times uttering hyperbole, and he had previously said for example that the year 2012 was "the mother of all years," and he had said that the release of iOS 10 was "the mother of all releases" – all of which does suggest he likes to use the handy "mother of" expression. But, I assure you, in terms of true self-driving cars, he has hit the nail on the head. For sure.

When you think about a moonshot and how we got to the moon, there are some identifiable characteristics and those same aspects can be applied to creating a true self-driving car. You'll notice that I keep putting the word "true" in front of the self-driving car expression. I do so because as per my essay about the various levels of self-driving cars, there are some self-driving cars that are only somewhat of a self-driving car. The somewhat versions are ones that require a human driver to be ready to intervene. In my view, that's not a true self-driving car. A true self-driving car is one that requires no human driver intervention at all. It is a car that can entirely undertake via automation the driving task without any human driver needed. This is the essence of what is known as a Level 5 self-driving car. We are currently at the Level 2 and Level 3 mark, and not yet at Level 5.

Getting to the moon involved aspects such as having big stretch goals, incremental progress, experimentation, innovation, and so on. Let's review how this applied to the moonshot of the bygone era, and how it applies to the self-driving car moonshot of today.

Big Stretch Goal

Trying to take a human and deliver the human to the moon, and bring them back, safely, was an extremely large stretch goal at the time. No one knew whether it could be done. The technology wasn't available yet. The cost was huge. The determination would need to be fierce. Etc. To reach a Level 5 self-driving car is going to be the same. It is a big stretch goal. We can readily get to the Level 3, and we are able to see the Level 4 just up ahead, but a Level 5 is still an unknown as to if it is doable. It should eventually be doable and in the same way that we thought we'd eventually get to the moon, but when it will occur is a different story.

Incremental Progress

Getting to the moon did not happen overnight in one fell swoop. It took years and years of incremental progress to get there. Likewise for self-driving cars. Google has famously been striving to get to the Level 5, and pretty much been willing to forgo dealing with the intervening levels, but most of the other self-driving car makers are doing the incremental route. Let's get a good Level 2 and a somewhat Level 3 going. Then, let's improve the Level 3 and get a somewhat Level 4 going. Then, let's improve the Level 4 and finally arrive at a Level 5. This seems to be the prevalent way that we are going to achieve the true self-driving car.

Experimentation

You likely know that there were various experiments involved in perfecting the approach and technology to get to the moon. As per making incremental progress, we first tried to see if we could get a rocket to go into space and safety return, then put a monkey in there, then with a human, then we went all the way to the moon but didn't land, and finally we arrived at the mission that actually landed on the moon. Self-driving cars are the same way. We are doing simulations of self-driving cars. We do testing of self-driving cars on private land under controlled situations. We do testing of self-driving cars on public roadways, often having to meet regulatory requirements including for example having an engineer or equivalent in the car to take over the controls if needed. And so on. Experiments big and small are needed to figure out what works and what doesn't.

Innovation

There are already some advances in AI that are allowing us to progress toward self-driving cars. We are going to need even more advances. Innovation in all aspects of technology are going to be required to achieve a true self-driving car. By no means do we already have everything in-hand that we need to get there. Expect new inventions and new approaches, new algorithms, etc.

Setbacks

Most of the pundits are avoiding talking about potential setbacks in the progress toward self-driving cars. Getting to the moon involved many setbacks, some of which you never have heard of and were buried at the time so as to not dampen enthusiasm and funding for getting to the moon. A recurring theme in many of my included essays is that there are going to be setbacks as we try to arrive at a true self-driving car. Take a deep breath and be ready. I just hope the setbacks don't completely stop progress. I am sure that it will cause progress to alter in a manner that we've not yet seen in the self-driving car field. I liken the self-driving car of today to the excitement everyone had for Uber when it first got going. Today, we have a different view of Uber and with each passing day there are more regulations to the ride sharing business and more concerns raised. The darling child only stays a darling until finally that child acts up. It will happen the same with self-driving cars.

SELF-DRIVING CARS CHALLENGES

But what exactly makes things so hard to have a true self-driving car, you might be asking. You have seen cruise control for years and years. You've lately seen cars that can do parallel parking. You've seen YouTube videos of Tesla drivers that put their hands out the window as their car zooms along the highway, and seen to therefore be in a self-driving car. Aren't we just needing to put a few more sensors onto a car and then we'll have in-hand a true self-driving car? Nope.

Consider for a moment the nature of the driving task. We don't just let anyone at any age drive a car. Worldwide, most countries won't license a driver until the age of 18, though many do allow a learner's permit at the age of 15 or 16. Some suggest that a younger age would be physically too small to reach the controls of the car. Though this might be the case, we could easily adjust the controls to allow for younger aged and thus smaller stature. It's not their physical size that matters. It's their cognitive development that matters.

To drive a car, you need to be able to reason about the car, what the car can and cannot do. You need to know how to operate the car. You need to know about how other cars on the road drive. You need to know what is allowed in driving such as speed limits and driving within marked lanes. You need to be able to react to situations and be able to avoid getting into accidents. You need to ascertain when to hit your brakes, when to steer clear of a pedestrian, and how to keep from ramming that motorcyclist that just cut you off.

Many of us had taken courses on driving. We studied about driving and took driver training. We had to take a test and pass it to be able to drive. The point being that though most adults take the driving task for granted, and we often "mindlessly" drive our cars, there is a significant amount of cognitive effort that goes into driving a car. After a while, it becomes second nature. You don't especially think about how you drive, you just do it. But, if you watch a novice driver, say a teenager learning to drive, you suddenly realize that there is a lot more complexity to it than we seem to realize.

Furthermore, driving is a very serious task. I recall when my daughter and son first learned to drive. They are both very conscientious people. They wanted to make sure that whatever they did, they did well, and that they did not harm anyone. Every day, when you get into a car, it is probably around 4,000 pounds of hefty metal and plastics (about two tons), and it is a lethal weapon. Think about it. You drive down the street in an object that weighs two tons and with the engine it can accelerate and ram into anything you want to hit. The damage a car can inflict is very scary. Both my children were surprised that they were being given the right to maneuver this monster of a beast that could cause tremendous harm entirely by merely letting go of the steering wheel for a moment or taking your eyes off the road.

In fact, in the United States alone there are about 30,000 deaths per year by auto accidents, which is around 100 per day. Given that there are about 263 million cars in the United States, I am actually more amazed that the number of fatalities is not a lot higher. During my morning commute, I look at all the thousands of cars on the freeway around me, and I think that if all of them decided to go zombie and drive in a crazy maniac way, there would be many people dead. Somehow, incredibly, each day, most people drive relatively safely. To me, that's a miracle right there. Getting millions and millions of people to be safe and sane when behind the wheel of a two ton mobile object, it's a feat that we as a society should admire with pride.

So, hopefully you are in agreement that the driving task requires a great deal of cognition. You don't' need to be especially smart to drive a car, and we've done quite a bit to make car driving viable for even the average dolt. There isn't an IQ test that you need to take to drive a car. If you can read and write, and pass a test, you pretty much can legally drive a car. There are of course some that drive a car and are not legally permitted to do so, plus there are private areas such as farms where drivers are young, but for public roadways in the United States, you can be generally of average intelligence (or less) and be able to legally drive.

This though makes it seem like the cognitive effort must not be much. If the cognitive effort was truly hard, wouldn't we only have Einstein's that could drive a car? We have made sure to keep the driving task as simple as we can, by making the controls easy and relatively standardized, and by having roads that are relatively standardized, and so on. It is as though Disneyland has put their Autopia into the real-world, by us all as a society agreeing that roads will be a certain way, and we'll all abide by the various rules of driving.

A modest cognitive task by a human is still something that stymies AI. You certainly know that AI has been able to beat chess players and be good at other kinds of games. This type of narrow cognition is not what car driving is about. Car driving is much wider. It requires knowledge about the world, which a chess playing AI system does not need to know. The cognitive aspects of driving are on the one hand seemingly simple, but at the same time require layer upon layer of knowledge about cars, people, roads, rules, and a myriad of other "common sense" aspects. We don't have any AI systems today that have that same kind of breadth and depth of awareness and knowledge.

As revealed in my essays, the self-driving car of today is using trickery to do particular tasks. It is all very narrow in operation. Plus, it currently assumes that a human driver is ready to intervene. It is like a child that we have taught to stack blocks, but we are needed to be right there in case the child stacks them too high and they begin to fall over. AI of today is brittle, it is narrow, and it does not approach the cognitive abilities of humans. This is why the true self-driving car is somewhere out in the future.

Another aspect to the driving task is that it is not solely a mind exercise. You do need to use your senses to drive. You use your eyes a vision sensors to see the road ahead. You vision capability is like a streaming video, which your brain needs to continually analyze as you drive. Where is the road? Is there a pedestrian in the way? Is there another car ahead of you? Your senses are relying a flood of info to your brain. Self-driving cars are trying to do the same, by using cameras, radar, ultrasound, and lasers. This is an attempt at mimicking how humans have senses and sensory apparatus.

Thus, the driving task is mental and physical. You use your senses, you use your arms and legs to manipulate the controls of the car, and you use your brain to assess the sensory info and direct your limbs to act upon the controls of the car. This all happens instantly. If you've ever perhaps gotten something in your eye and only had one eye available to drive with, you suddenly realize how dependent upon vision you are. If you have a broken foot with a cast, you suddenly realize how hard it is to control the brake pedal and the accelerator. If you've taken medication and your brain is maybe sluggish, you suddenly realize how much mental strain is required to drive a car.

An AI system that plays chess only needs to be focused on playing chess. The physical aspects aren't important because usually a human moves the chess pieces or the chessboard is shown on an electronic display. Using AI for a more life-and-death task such as analyzing MRI images of patients, this again does not require physical capabilities and instead is done by examining images of bits.

Driving a car is a true life-and-death task. It is a use of AI that can easily and at any moment produce death. For those colleagues of mine that are developing this AI, as am I, we need to keep in mind the somber aspects of this. We are producing software that will have in its virtual hands the lives of the occupants of the car, and the lives of those in other nearby cars, and the lives of nearby pedestrians, etc. Chess is not usually a life-or-death matter.

Driving is all around us. Cars are everywhere. Most of today's AI applications involve only a small number of people. Or, they are behind the scenes and we as humans have other recourse if the AI messes up. AI that is driving a car at 80 miles per hour on a highway had better not mess up. The consequences are grave. Multiply this by the number of cars, if we could put magically self-driving into every car in the USA, we'd have AI running in the 263 million cars. That's a lot of AI spread around. This is AI on a massive scale that we are not doing today and that offers both promise and potential peril.

There are some that want AI for self-driving cars because they envision a world without any car accidents. They envision a world in which there is no car congestion and all cars cooperate with each other. These are wonderful utopian visions.

They are also very misleading. The adoption of self-driving cars is going to be incremental and not overnight. We cannot economically just junk all existing cars. Nor are we going to be able to affordably retrofit existing cars. It is more likely that self-driving cars will be built into new cars and that over many years of gradual replacement of existing cars that we'll see the mix of self-driving cars become substantial in the real-world.

In these essays, I have tried to offer technological insights without being overly technical in my description, and also blended the business, societal, and economic aspects too. Technologists need to consider the non-technological impacts of what they do. Non-technologists should be aware of what is being developed.

We all need to work together to collectively be prepared for the enormous disruption and transformative aspects of true self-driving cars. We all need to be involved in this mother of all AI projects.

WHAT THIS BOOK PROVIDES

What does this book provide to you? It introduces many of the key elements about self-driving cars and does so with an AI based perspective. I weave together technical and non-technical aspects, readily going from being concerned about the cognitive capabilities of the driving task and how the technology is embodying this into self-driving cars, and in the next breath I discuss the societal and economic aspects.

They are all intertwined because that's the way reality is. You cannot separate out the technology per se, and instead must consider it within the milieu of what is being invented and innovated, and do so with a mindset towards the contemporary mores and culture that shape what we are doing and what we hope to do.

WHY THIS BOOK

I wrote this book to try and bring to the public view many aspects about self-driving cars that nobody seems to be discussing.

For business leaders that are either involved in making self-driving cars or that are going to leverage self-driving cars, I hope that this book will enlighten you as to the risks involved and ways in which you should be strategizing about how to deal with those risks.

For entrepreneurs, startups and other businesses that want to enter into the self-driving car market that is emerging, I hope this book sparks your interest in doing so, and provides some sense of what might be prudent to pursue.

For researchers that study self-driving cars, I hope this book spurs your interest in the risks and safety issues of self-driving cars, and also nudges you toward conducting research on those aspects.

For students in computer science or related disciplines, I hope this book will provide you with interesting and new ideas and material, for which you might conduct research or provide some career direction insights for you.

For AI companies and high-tech companies pursuing self-driving cars, this book will hopefully broaden your view beyond just the mere coding and development needed to make self-driving cars.

For all readers, I hope that you will find the material in this book to be stimulating. Some of it will be repetitive of things you already know. But I am pretty sure that you'll also find various eureka moments whereby you'll discover a new technique or approach that you had not earlier thought of. I am also betting that there will be material that forces you to rethink some of your current practices.

I am not saying you will suddenly have an epiphany and change what you are doing. I do think though that you will reconsider or perhaps revisit what you are doing.

For anyone choosing to use this book for teaching purposes, please take a look at my suggestions for doing so, as described in the Appendix. I have found the material handy in courses that I have taught, and likewise other faculty have told me that they have found the material handy, in some cases as extended readings and in other instances as a core part of their course (depending on the nature of the class).

In my writing for this book, I have tried carefully to blend both the practitioner and the academic styles of writing. It is not as dense as is typical academic journal writing, but at the same time offers depth by going into the nuances and trade-offs of various practices.

The word "deep" is in vogue today, meaning getting deeply into a subject or topic, and so is the word "unpack" which means to tease out the underlying aspects of a subject or topic. I have sought to offer material that addresses an issue or topic by going relatively deeply into it and make sure that it is well unpacked.

Finally, in any book about AI, it is difficult to use our everyday words without having some of them be misinterpreted. Specifically, it is easy to anthropomorphize AI. When I say that an AI system "knows" something, I do not want you to construe that the AI system has sentience and "knows" in the same way that humans do. They aren't that way, as yet. I have tried to use quotes around such words from time-to-time to emphasize that the words I am using should not be misinterpreted to ascribe true human intelligence to the AI systems that we know of today. If I used quotes around all such words, the book would be very difficult to read, and so I am doing so judiciously. Please keep that in mind as you read the material, thanks.

COMPANION BOOKS

If you find this material of interest, you might enjoy these too:

1. **"Introduction to Driverless Self-Driving Cars"** by Dr. Lance Eliot

2. **"Innovation and Thought Leadership on Self-Driving Driverless Cars"** by Dr. Lance Eliot

3. **"Advances in AI and Autonomous Vehicles: Cybernetic Self-Driving Cars"** by Dr. Lance Eliot

4. **"Self-Driving Cars: The Mother of All AI Projects"** by Dr. Lance Eliot

5. **"New Advances in AI Autonomous Driverless Self-Driving Cars"** by Dr. Lance Eliot

6. **"Autonomous Vehicle Driverless Self-Driving Cars and Artificial Intelligence"** by Dr. Lance Eliot and Michael B. Eliot

7. **"Transformative Artificial Intelligence Driverless Self-Driving Cars"** by Dr. Lance Eliot

8. **"Disruptive Artificial Intelligence and Driverless Self-Driving Cars"** by Dr. Lance Eliot

9. "State-of-the-Art AI Driverless Self-Driving Cars" by Dr. Lance Eliot

10. "Top Trends in AI Self-Driving Cars" by Dr. Lance Eliot

11. **"AI Innovations and Self-Driving Cars"** by Dr. Lance Eliot

12. **"Crucial Advances for AI Driverless Cars"** by Dr. Lance Eliot

13. **"Sociotechnical Insights and AI Driverless Cars"** by Dr. Lance Eliot.

14. **"Pioneering Advances for AI Driverless Cars"** by Dr. Lance Eliot

15. **"Leading Edge Trends for AI Driverless Cars"** by Dr. Lance Eliot

16. **"The Cutting Edge of AI Autonomous Cars"** by Dr. Lance Eliot

17. **"The Next Wave of AI Self-Driving Cars"** by Dr. Lance Eliot

18. **"Revolutionary Innovations of AI Driverless Cars"** by Dr. Lance Eliot

19. **"AI Self-Driving Cars Breakthroughs"** by Dr. Lance Eliot

20. **"Trailblazing Trends for AI Self-Driving Cars"** by Dr. Lance Eliot

21. **"Ingenious Strides for AI Driverless Cars"** by Dr. Lance Eliot

22. **"AI Self-Driving Cars Inventiveness"** by Dr. Lance Eliot

23. **"Visionary Secrets of AI Driverless Cars"** by Dr. Lance Eliot

These books are available on Amazon and at other major global booksellers.

CHAPTER 1

ELIOT FRAMEWORK FOR AI SELF-DRIVING CARS

CHAPTER 1

ELIOT FRAMEWORK FOR
AI SELF-DRIVING CARS

This chapter is a core foundational aspect for understanding AI self-driving cars and I have used this same chapter in several of my other books to introduce the reader to essential elements of this field. Once you've read this chapter, you'll be prepared to read the rest of the material since the foundational essence of the components of autonomous AI driverless self-driving cars will have been established for you.

––––––––––––

When I give presentations about self-driving cars and teach classes on the topic, I have found it helpful to provide a framework around which the various key elements of self-driving cars can be understood and organized (see diagram at the end of this chapter). The framework needs to be simple enough to convey the overarching elements, but at the same time not so simple that it belies the true complexity of self-driving cars. As such, I am going to describe the framework here and try to offer in a thousand words (or more!) what the framework diagram itself intends to portray.

The core elements on the diagram are numbered for ease of reference. The numbering does not suggest any kind of prioritization of the elements. Each element is crucial. Each element has a purpose, and otherwise would not be included in the framework. For some self-driving cars, a particular element might be more important or somehow distinguished in comparison to other self-driving cars.

You could even use the framework to rate a particular self-driving car, doing so by gauging how well it performs in each of the elements of the framework. I will describe each of the elements, one at a time. After doing so, I'll discuss aspects that illustrate how the elements interact and perform during the overall effort of a self-driving car.

At the Cybernetic Self-Driving Car Institute, we use the framework to keep track of what we are working on, and how we are developing software that fills in what is needed to achieve Level 5 self-driving cars.

D-01: Sensor Capture

Let's start with the one element that often gets the most attention in the press about self-driving cars, namely, the sensory devices for a self-driving car.

On the framework, the box labeled as D-01 indicates "Sensor Capture" and refers to the processes of the self-driving car that involve collecting data from the myriad of sensors that are used for a self-driving car. The types of devices typically involved are listed, such as the use of mono cameras, stereo cameras, LIDAR devices, radar systems, ultrasonic devices, GPS, IMU, and so on.

These devices are tasked with obtaining data about the status of the self-driving car and the world around it. Some of the devices are continually providing updates, while others of the devices await an indication by the self-driving car that the device is supposed to collect data. The data might be first transformed in some fashion by the device itself, or it might instead be fed directly into the sensor capture as raw data. At that point, it might be up to the sensor capture processes to do transformations on the data. This all varies depending upon the nature of the devices being used and how the devices were designed and developed.

D-02: Sensor Fusion

Imagine that your eyeballs receive visual images, your nose receives odors, your ears receive sounds, and in essence each of your distinct sensory devices is getting some form of input. The input befits the nature of the device. Likewise, for a self-driving car, the cameras provide visual images, the radar returns radar reflections, and so on.

Each device provides the data as befits what the device does.

At some point, using the analogy to humans, you need to merge together what your eyes see, what your nose smells, what your ears hear, and piece it all together into a larger sense of what the world is all about and what is happening around you. Sensor fusion is the action of taking the singular aspects from each of the devices and putting them together into a larger puzzle.

Sensor fusion is a tough task. There are some devices that might not be working at the time of the sensor capture. Or, there might some devices that are unable to report well what they have detected. Again, using a human analogy, suppose you are in a dark room and so your eyes cannot see much. At that point, you might need to rely more so on your ears and what you hear. The same is true for a self-driving car. If the cameras are obscured due to snow and sleet, it might be that the radar can provide a greater indication of what the external conditions consist of.

In the case of a self-driving car, there can be a plethora of such sensory devices. Each is reporting what it can. Each might have its difficulties. Each might have its limitations, such as how far ahead it can detect an object. All of these limitations need to be considered during the sensor fusion task.

D-03: Virtual World Model

For humans, we presumably keep in our minds a model of the world around us when we are driving a car. In your mind, you know that the car is going at say 60 miles per hour and that you are on a freeway. You have a model in your mind that your car is surrounded by other cars, and that there are lanes to the freeway. Your model is not only based on what you can see, hear, etc., but also what you know about the nature of the world. You know that at any moment that car ahead of you can smash on its brakes, or the car behind you can ram into your car, or that the truck in the next lane might swerve into your lane.

The AI of the self-driving car needs to have a virtual world model, which it then keeps updated with whatever it is receiving from the sensor fusion, which received its input from the sensor capture and the sensory devices.

D-04: System Action Plan

By having a virtual world model, the AI of the self-driving car is able to keep track of where the car is and what is happening around the car. In addition, the AI needs to determine what to do next. Should the self-driving car hit its brakes? Should the self-driving car stay in its lane or swerve into the lane to the left? Should the self-driving car accelerate or slow down?

A system action plan needs to be prepared by the AI of the self-driving car. The action plan specifies what actions should be taken. The actions need to pertain to the status of the virtual world model. Plus, the actions need to be realizable.

This realizability means that the AI cannot just assert that the self-driving car should suddenly sprout wings and fly. Instead, the AI must be bound by whatever the self-driving car can actually do, such as coming to a halt in a distance of X feet at a speed of Y miles per hour, rather than perhaps asserting that the self-driving car come to a halt in 0 feet as though it could instantaneously come to a stop while it is in motion.

D-05: Controls Activation

The system action plan is implemented by activating the controls of the car to act according to what the plan stipulates. This might mean that the accelerator control is commanded to increase the speed of the car. Or, the steering control is commanded to turn the steering wheel 30 degrees to the left or right.

One question arises as to whether or not the controls respond as they are commanded to do. In other words, suppose the AI has commanded the accelerator to increase, but for some reason it does not do so. Or, maybe it tries to do so, but the speed of the car does not increase. The controls activation feeds back into the virtual world model, and simultaneously the virtual world model is getting updated from the sensors, the sensor capture, and the sensor fusion. This allows the AI to ascertain what has taken place as a result of the controls being commanded to take some kind of action.

By the way, please keep in mind that though the diagram seems to have a linear progression to it, the reality is that these are all aspects of the self-driving car that are happening in parallel and simultaneously. The sensors are capturing data, meanwhile the sensor fusion is taking place, meanwhile the virtual model is being updated, meanwhile the system action plan is being formulated and reformulated, meanwhile the controls are being activated.

This is the same as a human being that is driving a car. They are eyeballing the road, meanwhile they are fusing in their mind the sights, sounds, etc., meanwhile their mind is updating their model of the world around them, meanwhile they are formulating an action plan of what to do, and meanwhile they are pushing their foot onto the pedals and steering the car. In the normal course of driving a car, you are doing all of these at once. I mention this so that when you look at the diagram, you will think of the boxes as processes that are all happening at the same time, and not as though only one happens and then the next.

They are shown diagrammatically in a simplistic manner to help comprehend what is taking place. You though should also realize that they are working in parallel and simultaneous with each other. This is a tough aspect in that the inter-element communications involve latency and other aspects that must be taken into account. There can be delays in one element updating and then sharing its latest status with other elements.

D-06: Automobile & CAN

Contemporary cars use various automotive electronics and a Controller Area Network (CAN) to serve as the components that underlie the driving aspects of a car. There are Electronic Control Units (ECU's) which control subsystems of the car, such as the engine, the brakes, the doors, the windows, and so on.

The elements D-01, D-02, D-03, D-04, D-05 are layered on top of the D-06, and must be aware of the nature of what the D-06 is able to do and not do.

D-07: In-Car Commands

Humans are going to be occupants in self-driving cars. In a Level 5 self-driving car, there must be some form of communication that takes place between the humans and the self-driving car. For example, I go into a self-driving car and tell it that I want to be driven over to Disneyland, and along the way I want to stop at In-and-Out Burger. The self-driving car now parses what I've said and tries to then establish a means to carry out my wishes.

In-car commands can happen at any time during a driving journey. Though my example was about an in-car command when I first got into my self-driving car, it could be that while the self-driving car is carrying out the journey that I change my mind. Perhaps after getting stuck in traffic, I tell the self-driving car to forget about getting the burgers and just head straight over to the theme park. The self-driving car needs to be alert to in-car commands throughout the journey.

D-08: V2X Communications

We will ultimately have self-driving cars communicating with each other, doing so via V2V (Vehicle-to-Vehicle) communications. We will also have self-driving cars that communicate with the roadways and other aspects of the transportation infrastructure, doing so via V2I (Vehicle-to-Infrastructure).

The variety of ways in which a self-driving car will be communicating with other cars and infrastructure is being called V2X, whereby the letter X means whatever else we identify as something that a car should or would want to communicate with. The V2X communications will be taking place simultaneous with everything else on the diagram, and those other elements will need to incorporate whatever it gleans from those V2X communications.

D-09: Deep Learning

The use of Deep Learning permeates all other aspects of the self-driving car. The AI of the self-driving car will be using deep learning to do a better job at the systems action plan, and at the controls activation, and at the sensor fusion, and so on.

Currently, the use of artificial neural networks is the most prevalent form of deep learning. Based on large swaths of data, the neural networks attempt to "learn" from the data and therefore direct the efforts of the self-driving car accordingly.

D-10: Tactical AI

Tactical AI is the element of dealing with the moment-to-moment driving of the self-driving car. Is the self-driving car staying in its lane of the freeway? Is the car responding appropriately to the controls commands? Are the sensory devices working?

For human drivers, the tactical equivalent can be seen when you watch a novice driver such as a teenager that is first driving. They are focused on the mechanics of the driving task, keeping their eye on the road while also trying to properly control the car.

D-11: Strategic AI

The Strategic AI aspects of a self-driving car are dealing with the larger picture of what the self-driving car is trying to do. If I had asked that the self-driving car take me to Disneyland, there is an overall journey map that needs to be kept and maintained.

There is an interaction between the Strategic AI and the Tactical AI. The Strategic AI is wanting to keep on the mission of the driving, while the Tactical AI is focused on the particulars underway in the driving effort. If the Tactical AI seems to wander away from the overarching mission, the Strategic AI wants to see why and get things back on track. If the Tactical AI realizes that there is something amiss on the self-driving car, it needs to alert the Strategic AI accordingly and have an adjustment to the overarching mission that is underway.

D-12: Self-Aware AI

Very few of the self-driving cars being developed are including a Self-Aware AI element, which we at the Cybernetic Self-Driving Car Institute believe is crucial to Level 5 self-driving cars.

The Self-Aware AI element is intended to watch over itself, in the sense that the AI is making sure that the AI is working as intended. Suppose you had a human driving a car, and they were starting to drive erratically. Hopefully, their own self-awareness would make them realize they themselves are driving poorly, such as perhaps starting to fall asleep after having been driving for hours on end. If you had a passenger in the car, they might be able to alert the driver if the driver is starting to do something amiss. This is exactly what the Self-Aware

AI element tries to do, it becomes the overseer of the AI, and tries to detect when the AI has become faulty or confused, and then find ways to overcome the issue.

D-13: Economic

The economic aspects of a self-driving car are not per se a technology aspect of a self-driving car, but the economics do indeed impact the nature of a self-driving car. For example, the cost of outfitting a self-driving car with every kind of possible sensory device is prohibitive, and so choices need to be made about which devices are used. And, for those sensory devices chosen, whether they would have a full set of features or a more limited set of features.

We are going to have self-driving cars that are at the low-end of a consumer cost point, and others at the high-end of a consumer cost point. You cannot expect that the self-driving car at the low-end is going to be as robust as the one at the high-end. I realize that many of the self-driving car pundits are acting as though all self-driving cars will be the same, but they won't be. Just like anything else, we are going to have self-driving cars that have a range of capabilities. Some will be better than others. Some will be safer than others. This is the way of the real-world, and so we need to be thinking about the economics aspects when considering the nature of self-driving cars.

D-14: Societal

This component encompasses the societal aspects of AI which also impacts the technology of self-driving cars. For example, the famous Trolley Problem involves what choices should a self-driving car make when faced with life-and-death matters. If the self-driving car is about to either hit a child standing in the roadway, or instead ram into a tree at the side of the road and possibly kill the humans in the self-driving car, which choice should be made?

We need to keep in mind the societal aspects will underlie the AI of the self-driving car. Whether we are aware of it explicitly or not, the AI will have embedded into it various societal assumptions.

D-15: Innovation

I included the notion of innovation into the framework because we can anticipate that whatever a self-driving car consists of, it will continue to be innovated over time. The self-driving cars coming out in the next several years will undoubtedly be different and less innovative than the versions that come out in ten years hence, and so on.

Framework Overall

For those of you that want to learn about self-driving cars, you can potentially pick a particular element and become specialized in that aspect. Some engineers are focusing on the sensory devices. Some engineers focus on the controls activation. And so on. There are specialties in each of the elements.

Researchers are likewise specializing in various aspects. For example, there are researchers that are using Deep Learning to see how best it can be used for sensor fusion. There are other researchers that are using Deep Learning to derive good System Action Plans. Some are studying how to develop AI for the Strategic aspects of the driving task, while others are focused on the Tactical aspects.

A well-prepared all-around software developer that is involved in self-driving cars should be familiar with all of the elements, at least to the degree that they know what each element does. This is important since whatever piece of the pie that the software developer works on, they need to be knowledgeable about what the other elements are doing.

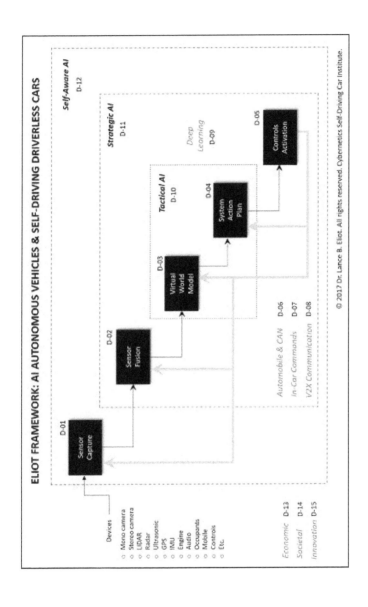

CHAPTER 2

SEAT BELTS
AND
AI SELF-DRIVING CARS

CHAPTER 2

SEAT BELTS
AND AI SELF-DRIVING CARS

Seat belts. Some people love them and feel reassured to be wearing one while inside a moving car. Others hate them and feel trapped, at times even trying to find clever ways to avoid wearing them. Most of us now know that as a driver you ought to be wearing your seat belt, and for which modern day cars will usually put up quite a holler if you aren't wearing one.

I remember my grandparents telling me when I was young that they normally did not wear a seat belt. They indicated too that when Congress passed the Federal Motor Vehicle Safety law in the mid-1960s making seat belts mandatory in cars, they nearly went to Washington DC to protest. Indeed, they defiantly refused to wear seat belts at all, and made a proud show of disdain for seat belts every time they got into a car.

They had experienced primarily lap belts for most of their driving life. I vividly recall them buckling all of the lap belts that were in the car and telling any passengers to sit atop the buckled seat belt. Buckling the seat belts was partially to satisfy the system that later on was able to detect whether a seat belt was fastened or not, and they also did it to overtly carry out their protest. If the seat belts were unbuckled, it could be that you didn't even realize they were there. For them, by buckling the seat belts, and purposely sitting on top of them, it was an indicator that you knew what you are doing and did so for a reason.

The 3-point belt standard got them further riled up. The early versions were someone confusing to use and this added more fuel to the fire as to why they were necessary and seemed primarily to be there as an annoyance. How do these darned things work, they would exclaim? Stupidly designed, not needed, abhorrent, they would say.

It really galled them when seat belts were added to the backseat of cars. They somewhat begrudgingly could understand the basis for putting seat belts in the front seats of a car, particularly for the driver, but it was unfathomable to put them into the backseat. Who in the world would want or need to wear seat belts while in the backseat? It became an open secret that they were convinced that the seat belt manufacturers had a monopoly going on and had in a conspiratorial manner kowtowed the government into keeping them in business by insisting on seat belts throughout a car.

At times, my beloved grandparents would sit in the back seat of my car, once I was older and able to drive, and would explain to me that the reason they did not need to wear a seat belt in the backseat was that they were strong enough to hang-on if anything happened while the car was in motion. This became a test of their personal strength as elders, suggesting that if they were too weak to hang onto an armrest or steady themselves if the car swerved, it somehow implied they were weak of mind, body, and spirit.

In their latter years, air bags were just coming to fruition, which was mainly during the 1970s and the 1980s. I almost shouldn't tell you what they thought of air bags. The good news is that at first they thought air bags were the best thing since sliced bread. In their minds, having air bags meant you for sure did not need to wear your seat belt. This was of course in contrast to the clearly indicated aspect that you were supposed to wear your seat belt and that the air bag was merely a supplemental form of safety restraint.

Nope, for them, the air bag was the kiss-of-death to the need for seat belts. They assumed that the air bag would save them in any kind of incident. They weren't sure how the contraptions worked and figured it was a compressed down-filed pillow that somehow expanded and gave your head and body a soft place to land. I suppose you could somewhat excuse them on this misunderstanding, given that the auto makers initially referred to the air bag as an Air Cushion Restraint System (ACRS), which sounds kind of like a pillow, I suppose.

My grandparents weren't around when air bags began to become not only standard but also you'd have several of them, perhaps six or more, outfitted into a conventional car. I'd dare say that they'd be once again threatening to protest in Washington DC about this proliferation of air bags. Why, you might ask, since they had initially hailed the invention of air bags?

You might not know that when air bags were first being deployed, even some of the major auto makers opposed them, including Ford and GM, doing so under the claim that air bags were inappropriate and lacked consumer demand. There were also rumors of air bags that suddenly deployed on their own and either scared the dickens out of the driver or caused the driver to lose control of the car. There were rumors that the air bags would injure you upon deployment and you were at as much risk in not more so of death from the air bag as you would be from the car getting into a collision.

Though some of those rumors were baseless, there is still to this day controversy associated with air bags. The National Highway Traffic Safety Administration (NHTSA) did a study in the early 2000s and found that over a twelve-year period there were over 200 deaths due to air bags. The deaths occurred at low speeds and the NHTSA said that the air bag was the more likely culprit of the death than due to the underlying incident that led to the deployment of the air bag. For higher speeds, they could not readily differentiate what led to a death and so tended to not attribute deaths to the air bags when the incident involved high speeds.

Getting back to the topic of seat belts, I'm happy to say that my children are quite inured to the use of seat belts. They would not even consider driving a car without wearing seat belts and will nearly always urge others in their cars to be wearing their seat belts. Of course, you could say that they've grown-up with seat belts and it was the constant drumbeat during their generation that aided them in becoming seat belt advocates. My grandparents had obviously grown-up in a different era and perceived seat belts in a radically different way.

One aspect that I never could fully grasp about my grandparents' concerns was that they insisted the seat belt would hamper the driving of a car. I don't know about you, but I've never had a situation that I thought my seat belt got in the way of my driving the car. Certainly, I've had a number of moments when the belt tension mounted and became uncomfortable taut due to a rapid maneuver. I didn't find myself though unable to maintain control of the driving task. You might suggest it helped me maintain control since I would have otherwise likely had my body and limbs flailed around.

Another qualm they had was that the seat belt could end-up killing you. Have you heard that one before? You might be puzzled about killer seat belts. Let me enlighten you.

My grandparents asserted that you might get into a car accident and not be able to escape from the car. The seat belt would keep you pinned into the wrecked car. They were convinced that the chances of you getting stuck inside a burning car was far more likely than whatever other protection or safety that the seat belt offered. In a risk-reward equation, they argued that putting on a seat belt was like a death sentence, meaning that if the car got into an accident you would be a dead person. They, meanwhile, free of the seat belt as a restraint, would walk or crawl out of the burning car and survive.

What amplified their claim were movies and TV shows that would vividly depict a car plunging dramatically into a body of water such as an ocean or a lake, and the person inside the car would be trapped by their seat belt and drown (a surprisingly frequent plot device in murder mysteries and James Bond spy stories).

Living near an ocean here in Southern California seemingly put me at heightened risk, and when they realized that we also have parks with small lakes, well, this was enough to get them to plead with me to not wear my seat belt. I bought one of those seat belts cutting tools, which also doubled as a tool to break the glass of the windshield, hoping this would ease their concerns. It did not.

By the way, I've never managed to drive my car into the ocean or into a lake, and nor even into a swimming pool. I might be living on borrowed time. Yes, I still keep the handy escape tool in my car, as per the lessons of life handed down to me by my grandparents.

I trust that you know that the odds of seat belts "killing" you are exceedingly remote. I won't say it is zero odds, which maybe you might assume, at the same time I think using whatever the tiny rate might be as a basis for overlooking the safety of wearing the seat belt, well, it's an easy calculation. Wear your seat belt.

In California, it is the law that you must wear your seat belt. And it is not just the driver that must wear a seat belt. The law here is that the driver and all passengers in a car that are over the age of 8 or are children sized 4 feet 9 inches tall or taller must all be wearing seat belts. This encompasses whenever you are driving on public roads. It also applies to private property, including parking lots and in other circumstances. Children that are younger than the stated threshold or smaller than the stated threshold must be in federally-approved child car seat restraints.

In some states, the police can stop you if you are not wearing a seat belt, allowing them to share with you the importance of wearing a seat belt and you can get a ticket for not having worn it. Other states don't permit the police to stop you for not wearing seat belts, considering it not serious enough to warrant a police stop, though if you are stopped for some other valid reason, the police can then cite you for the lack of wearing seat belts.

I know one couple that was visiting here in California and got a bit upset when they had gently rolled through a stop sign and the police stopped them (they acknowledged this was wrong to do), and subsequently the police noticed that their teenage children in the back seat were not wearing seat belts and cited the driver for each of those offenses.

The driver was a bit steamed and argued that they should not be held responsible for what the teenagers in the backseat were doing.

What was he supposed to have done? Well, here in California, any passenger under the age of 16 that is not wearing a seat belt will mean that the driver gets the blame (or, more properly stated, has the responsibility, which the driver should have duly exercised and made sure the teens were wearing seat belts, akin to being the captain of a ship).

When I was in college, I had a friend that drove a beat-up old jalopy of a car. It was in pretty bad shape. He had seat belts in the car. These were the most dilapidated seat belts I had ever seen. He said he couldn't afford to replace them.

As frayed as these seat belts were, I was sure that in an accident they would immediately be torn apart at their loose ends and the belts would not hold in anyone or anything of any substantive weight or size. He was lucky that he never got stopped by the police. If a police officer had seen those seat belts, it would have been tickets galore, since it's another law here that your seat belts must be in proper working order. He was doubly lucky that he never got into an actual incident severe enough to require the seat belts to work as expected.

In case this discussion about seat belts has not been clear cut, let me point out that seat belts will generally increase your chances of surviving car crashes or other such incidents, at least more so than if you aren't wearing the seat belts. Of course, the seat belts need to be in proper shape. You also need to wear them the right way. If you goof around and aren't wearing the seat belts as intended, you are defeating their purpose, plus it can cause you added injury during an incident, such as to your spine or torso.

For the driver of a car, the seat belt can aid them in being able to retain control of the driving task. Whereas they might be tossed around wildly without seat belts, the intent is that you'll stay pretty much in place and be able to therefore continue to access the steering wheel and the pedals. This staying in place might allow you to drive your way out of whatever predicament is taking place or at least perhaps be able to more safely consider other drivable options.

It can also aid in reducing the severity of the whipping motions and might prevent your body from otherwise damage that it could sustain due to the incident by not wearing seat belts.

Front seat passengers can also gain advantages by wearing their seat belts. A front seat passenger that is not wearing a seat belt can inadvertently get tossed into the driver of the car, causing the driver to lose control of the car or perhaps leading to the driver hitting the gas or steering radically when they didn't intend to do so. The front seat passenger could get launched through the front windshield in a severe impact of the car hitting another car or ramming into something, which would likely not occur if the person was wearing a seat belt.

The backseat seat belts are for many people less essential, since they assume that anyone in the backseat will somehow be magically okay in a car incident. Those people falsely think that whatever happens in the backseat won't affect the front seat and the driving. Little do they seem to know that a person flying around in a backseat can readily push into the back of a front seat, causing havoc to the driver sitting in the front seat. It is even possible for the person in the backseat to go flying up into the front seat of the car, or possibly get launched through the front windshield.

There is also the aspect that while in the backseat, you likely don't want to be flailing around loosely, even if you don't happen to knock into the front seat of the car. Imagine if say two people are sitting in the backseat. There's a rapid car movement which is going to cause a hard braking or swerving of the car. These two people can be tossed around like rag dolls and hit each other, including causing broken bones or worse. If they had been wearing their seat belts, they might have still bumped somewhat into each other, but the likely injuries are going to be less severe.

Some recent studies about the wearing of seat belts has indicated that people often do not wear the backseat seat belts when they get into a ridesharing car.

These are people that would normally wear their seat belts in the backseat of a car of someone that they knew. But, when they get into a ridesharing car, they often do not put on the backseat seat belts.

The news media seemed puzzled by this matter. I think it seems quite obvious. When you get into a ridesharing car, you are likely going to take a very short trip, and you are assuming that the chances of a car incident occurring are low, due to the short distance and time involved in the travel. You are also likely used to getting into vehicles such as busses that often do not have seat belts.

There is also the matter of figuring out the seat belts in a car that you are not familiar with. This might seem ridiculous since all seat belts are pretty much the same. All I can say is that I've seen people struggle mightily with the seat belts while in the backseat of cars. They mentally might be calculating that the amount of time required to figure out the seat belt and put it on exceeds the amount of time they are going to be in the ridesharing car.

Some might also ascribe a level of proficiency to the ridesharing driver. These passengers might believe that the ridesharing driver is a professional driver and so less likely to get involved into an incident, perhaps more so than would someone that they know as a friend or colleague. I'm not going to put too much stock into that part of the theory. There are some that go the opposite direction on this belief in the sense that they assume that since the ridesharing driver is on the road so much of the time, the odds are they are going to ultimately get into incidents that others that don't spend as much time on the road will not.

In any case, the recent spate of news coverage has brought to the forefront a number of popular YouTube videos that showcase what can happen when you are in a ridesharing car that gets into an incident. If you want to scare yourself into forever putting on your seat belt while a passenger, go ahead and watch one of those videos. Maybe get others that you know to watch the videos too, since it will heighten their understanding of how a human being can become an unguided missile while sitting in the back of a car.

I don't want to sound like some kind of seatbelt crazed advocate. I am not suggesting that seat belts are a cure all. They are a reasoned form of safety that has tradeoffs. Yes, bad things can happen while wearing a seat belt. Likewise, bad things can happen with air bags. For now, these bad things are generally outweighed by the good things that these safety features provide. It is not an absolute. It is the calculation of risk-reward and for which the seat belt is more of a plus than a negative.

In the case of air bags, there's not much choice per se that you have about those. If your car is equipped with them, they are either going to deploy or not, and either help you or not. Some cars have plenty of them, some cars have very few or none at all (in the USA, cars sold after 1998 became required to be equipped with air bags for the front seats of the car). Some cars also allow you to disable the air bags. Overall, the air bags "choice" for a driver or passenger is not particularly a choice as much as it is a given, while the use of seat belts is more so a type of choice, one might argue.

What does this have to do with AI self-driving cars?

At the Cybernetic AI Self-Driving Car Institute, we are developing AI software for self-driving cars. One aspect to consider is the nature and use of safety restraints such as seat belts and air bags. I often get asked whether or not we'll still have such constraints in a world of AI self-driving cars.

Allow me to elaborate.

I'd like to first clarify and introduce the notion that there are varying levels of AI self-driving cars. The topmost level is considered Level 5. A Level 5 self-driving car is one that is being driven by the AI and there is no human driver involved. For the design of Level 5 self-driving cars, the auto makers are even removing the gas pedal, brake pedal, and steering wheel, since those are contraptions used by human drivers. The Level 5 self-driving car is not being driven by a human and nor is there an expectation that a human driver will be present in the self-driving car. It's all on the shoulders of the AI to drive the car.

For self-driving cars less than a Level 5, there must be a human driver present in the car. The human driver is currently considered the responsible party for the acts of the car. The AI and the human driver are co-sharing the driving task. In spite of this co-sharing, the human is supposed to remain fully immersed into the driving task and be ready at all times to perform the driving task. I've repeatedly warned about the dangers of this co-sharing arrangement and predicted it will produce many untoward results.

Let's focus herein on the true Level 5 self-driving car. Much of the comments apply to the less than Level 5 self-driving cars too, but the fully autonomous AI self-driving car will receive the most attention in this discussion.

Here's the usual steps involved in the AI driving task:

- Sensor data collection and interpretation
- Sensor fusion
- Virtual world model updating
- AI action planning
- Car controls command issuance

Another key aspect of AI self-driving cars is that they will be driving on our roadways in the midst of human driven cars too. There are some pundits of AI self-driving cars that continually refer to a utopian world in which there are only AI self-driving cars on the public roads. Currently there are about 250+ million conventional cars in the United States alone, and those cars are not going to magically disappear or become true Level 5 AI self-driving cars overnight.

Indeed, the use of human driven cars will last for many years, likely many decades, and the advent of AI self-driving cars will occur while there are still human driven cars on the roads. This is a crucial point since this means that the AI of self-driving cars needs to be able to contend with not just other AI self-driving cars, but also contend with human driven cars. It is easy to envision a simplistic and rather unrealistic world in which all AI self-driving cars are politely interacting with each other and being civil about roadway interactions. That's not what is going to be happening for the foreseeable future. AI self-driving cars and human driven cars will need to be able to cope with each other.

Returning to the topic of safety restraints, let's consider what might happen as a result of the advent of AI self-driving cars.

First, let's consider the self-driving cars that are less than Level 5.

Those less-than-Level 5 AI self-driving cars will need a human licensed driver at the wheel and the human driver must be ready to take over the driving task when needed. In many respects, this is no different than being in a conventional car in the sense that the human driver should be snugly in their driver's seat and be kept in place via a seat belt, along with having air bags at the ready. So, everything I've just mentioned about the importance of a driver wearing a seat belt applies equally to the less-than-Level 5 AI self-driving cars.

There is a bit of twist though.

One issue that I've repeatedly brought up about the Level 3 and Level 4 self-driving cars is that the human driver is likely to become disjointed from the driving task.

As the automation gets better and better, there is a tendency for a human driver to become increasingly careless and aloof of the driving effort. This is a highly dangerous circumstance since the odds are that the human driver will be needed immediately if the AI opts to handover the driving to the human driver, and yet the human driver might be mentally adrift of the driving situation.

In addition to being mentally adrift, there is a high chance that the human driver will be physically adrift too.

You've perhaps seen videos of human drivers reading a book, texting on their smartphones, and otherwise physically having their limbs away from the controls of the car. These human drivers often will also shift their body and be angled towards the front seat passenger or perhaps be turned slightly backwards to look at the passengers in the backseat.

Whereas in a conventional car the preponderance of drivers tend to realize that they need to keep their body and limbs within close proximity of the driving controls, the temptation of the heightened automation in a Level 3 and Level 4 will prompt them to be adrift of the car pedals and steering wheel.

This raises the question of whether or not we'll potentially see more human drivers that will seek to avoid their seat belts or misuse the seat belt by not remaining in place. I would anticipate that we'll see a lot of human drivers that allow themselves to get into such a predicament. They might upon initial foray into using a Level 3 or Level 4 self-driving car be closely attentive to remaining well-connected with the driving controls, but over time, inexorably, if nothing adverse seems to occur, they will stretch out their physical boundaries.

For seat belts, it means that the seat belt will not be as protective as normally expected. Is this due to a design issue of the seat belt or is it due to the "misuse" by the human driver?

You could try to place all the blame and responsibility onto the inattentive human driver. That's the easy way out. I'd like to suggest that we instead consider how to use automation and the AI to help on the matter.

There is already a move afoot to use cameras that are inward facing to watch the human driver and alert them when they are no longer looking ahead at the roadway. These cameras can also scan the position of the eyes of the human driver, thus, their head needs to be straight ahead, and their eyes need to be looking ahead too. There are new devices on steering wheels to detect whether the driver has their hands on the wheel and if they are away from it too long the steering wheel lights up or a sound or some alert warns them about this.

We can use the AI to bring together the array of sensory data about the human driver and use it in a coordinated manner to have the AI discuss with the human driver the need to remain involved in the driving efforts. Rather than merely a series of beeps and lights that go on, it would be handy to leverage the socio-behavioral Natural Language Processing (NLP) capabilities of the on-board AI system to inspire the human driver and keep them engaged in the driving task.

The seat belt and the physical position of the human driver can also be scanned via the inward facing cameras. This would allow the AI to further determine how far away from the driving controls the human driver is becoming, along with whether the human driver is putting themselves into greater danger by not being in the proper placement for the seat belt to work as intended.

As an aside, this same use of the camera data can be helpful in ensuring that the human driver remains well-positioned related to the air bags that are nearby to the driver's position. Many people seem completely unaware that they can be dangerously harmed if they are too close to an air bag when it deploys. The recommended distance is about 10 inches away from the inflation point, which is usually easily found at the location of the airbag cover. This distance could be monitored by the AI system and the human driver notified when they have become to close (and also warn when they are to distant).

There are numerous research efforts underway to create the next-generation of seat belts, which some are referring to as Smart Seat Belts (SSB's).

These advanced versions of seat belts have embedded sensors. Those sensors would become another form of data collection for the AI system and allow it to ascertain the placement related to the driver. In this manner, not only would there be the visual data from the inward facing camera, but in addition there would be data coming from the seat belt itself.

It is anticipated that the SSB's would provide a kind of customization for the wearer of the seat belt. The seat belt would contain elements that could allow it to stretch and extend, or tighten and become more fitting, depending upon the size and weight of the human driver.

Hopefully, this would act as another form of encouragement for the human driver to make sure they are wearing their seat belt and doing so in the appropriate manner.

For a Level 3 or Level 4 AI self-driving car, I've emphasized herein that the human driver must remain involved and aware of the driving task, and that the use of the seat belt is crucial in that effort. The AI can help to keep track of the position of the human driver and perhaps by using NLP talk the human driver into being more compliant. I say this because I'd bet that beeps and lights would not be quite as effective as a disembodied AI savvy voice that politely and yet sternly acts as a reminder of the right thing to be doing.

What about the passengers in the Level 3 and Level 4 self-driving car?

I'll extend my remarks about the driver to suggest that we can have the AI be detecting the positions of the passengers too, and once again trying to inspire them to also properly wear their seat belts. The inward facing camera will readily be able to see the front seat passengers, and it is likely that the camera would also be able to see the backseat passengers, or there might be additional cameras throughout the interior to make sure that the backseat passengers can also be seen.

Perhaps the parent in the driver seat will no longer need to be "the tough parent" and have to ask or insist that those teens in the backseat put on their seat belts. The AI can take on that role. The parent would either shrug their shoulders and say it's the AI way or no way, or the parent would hopefully acknowledge the helpfulness of the AI in providing a handy reminder about the importance of wearing seat belts. One does have to have sympathy that any hectic parent can easily neglect to keep in mind the importance of seat belts. I've pointed out earlier that this can be a serious omission of ensuring that that those backseat passengers aren't going to become flying projectiles.

Let's now turn our attention to the Level 5 self-driving cars.

In a Level 5 self-driving car, there is no need to have a human driver present. If one happens to be in the Level 5 self-driving car, it is not especially noteworthy since there are unlikely to be any driving controls inside the Level 5 self-driving car anyway. As such, all those humans inside the Level 5 self-driving car are passengers, regardless of whether they are adults or children, and regardless of any kind of driving prowess they each might have.

Here's where things get really tricky.

It has been predicted that the interior of Level 5 AI self-driving cars will be radically different than the interior of today's conventional cars. One of the main reasons to redo the interior is that there is no longer a need to have the driving controls, which normally takes up a chunk of space at the front of the interior. Likewise, there is no need to have a driver's seat.

The car interior now becomes a freed-up space that can be used for whatever you want it to be used for.

Some auto makers are possibly going to be put swivel seats that allow the passengers to face each other, or not, as they might wish to swivel back-and-forth during a driving journey. There are auto makers that are going to be putting recliners into the car, or perhaps even beds. The thinking is that people will start using their cars to take them on longer trips and will want to sleep in their car. Or, maybe during their morning commute to work they might want to take a brief nap.

This is exciting and will utterly change our perception of the use of a car interior.

I'll bring us all back to earth and point out that whatever you do in this interior space, you still need to have safety restraints. Sorry about that, I hope this didn't burst anyone's bubble.

I've seen some concept designs of car interiors that omit entirely any kind of seat belts. I know that a concept design is supposed to look sleek and sexy, but I have a bit of concern about not showing the seat belts. You might say it's a small omission and not worthy of noting. I guess we'll disagree on that point. I don't want people having false expectations that they will now be suddenly rid of seat belts.

Indeed, when I speak at AI industry conferences, it does seem that a lot of people falsely believe that there will be no need for any safety restraints, and certainly not seat belts.

Why is this?

I'll start with the point that makes me aghast. I have some people that say there will never be any car accidents once we have all AI self-driving cars. This is some magical notion that the AI self-driving cars will all carefully coordinate their actions and we'll never again have any kind of car collisions. This is some wild kind of dreamworld that these people have bought into.

The first aspect is that there will be an ongoing mix of both AI self-driving cars and human driven cars for quite a while, maybe forever, and thus there is not going to be this Utopian world of solely AI self-driving cars (as I had mentioned earlier herein). You had best face the facts. And, in that case, we are going to have car collisions and impacts with other cars, presumably mainly AI self-driving cars and human driven cars making adverse contact with each other.

Even if we somehow removed all human driven cars from the roadways, and we had only AI self-driving cars, explain to me what an AI self-driving car is going to do when a dog rushes out into the street from behind a large tree. The physics of the situation are going to be that the AI self-driving car will need to hit its brakes. For those of you that counter-argue that the AI should have detected the dog beforehand, I defy you to be able to offer any means by which all such "surprises" will be eliminated from the world of driving as know it. A dog hidden behind a tree is not something that can be so readily detected.

This brings up another point about being inside a car. You are not wearing seat belts only because of car accidents. Whenever the driver of a car has to hit the brakes, or maybe take a curve very fast, or perform other such maneuvers, the humans inside the car are going to be tossed back-and-forth. The seat belts are used for that safety purpose too. It's not just when there is an actual car accident that the seat belts come to play.

You might not give much thought to all that your seat belt does for you in any given driving journey. I would wager that if we put a sensor onto your seat belt and it kept track of how many times it helped restrain you, for just your daily commute to work, we'd likely see that the seat belt is a silent but crucial form of safety for you.

How will safety belts function when you are in a swivel seat of your fancy new Level 5 AI self-driving car?

Do we need a new kind of seat belt?

Will people be upset that their seat belts restrain them, which maybe right now they don't notice as much, but when they are wanting to move around in those swivel seats it could become a more apparent matter.

I'd also guess that people will be tempted to take off their seat belts. Currently, in a conventional car interior, if you take off your seat belt, there's not much else you can do anyway, and so why bother to remove it. In the case of the car interior for Level 5 AI self-driving cars, you might be using the interior to play games or do something else that you'd prefer to be freed-up and not have to remain in your seated position and restrained by the seat belt.

You can also imagine the difficulty now of having air bags inside the Level 5 AI self-driving car. Where will the human be and what is their position? Will the air bag deploy in a manner that befits the position of the human passenger?

With a conventional car, you are pretty much guaranteed where the humans will be seated. This makes it relatively easy to position the air bags. In a Level 5 AI self-driving car, the humans will have additional flexibility in terms of where they will be seated, their angle, their pitch, and so on.

This becomes a kind of moving target and not easy to make sure an air bag will be of help to them when needed (and not a danger either).

If the humans are reclining, we once again need to identify what kind of seat belt can aid them. The same is the case with full-on prone position for sleeping inside a moving car. I suppose you might right away be saying that trains allow you to sleep on-board and you don't need to wear a seat belt. Cruise ships let you sleep without a seat belt. Airplanes generally let you sleep without a seat belt or they tell you to go ahead and keep it loosely around you, and also be ready to awaken if prompted and then sit up and make sure your seat belt is properly on you.

Of course, the answer is that a moving car is not the same as an airplane, nor the same as a cruise ship, nor the same as train. I hope you see that's apparent. Its closest cousin would be a bus. Most overnight busses admittedly let you sleep on-board without any specialized seat belt, though many would say this is a loophole in the rules and endangers people. Perhaps the low number of miles driven while sleeping in a bus is little enough that no one wants to hassle it, plus, the thinking is that a bus is big and not perhaps as prone to coming to sudden stops or getting into accidents.

The vast number of miles that people will be going in their Level 5 AI self-driving cars, along with the aspect that these are cars, meaning they are relatively smaller than a bus and more likely to have severe consequences to the occupants when something untoward happens, it all adds up that we'll need to have specialized seat belts for dealing with being inside these self-driving cars. And, we'll need to encourage passengers to use those seat belts.

It is anticipated that the Level 5 AI self-driving cars will become the mainstay of the ridesharing cars. If that's the case, should the AI act as an "enforcer" and get those that are riding in a ridesharing car to put on their seat belts and keep those seat belts on? I mention this because there won't be a human driver in the ridesharing car that could suggest it to the passengers. It would seem to be up to the AI to do something about this.

I realize that when I suggest that the AI should be informing passengers about their seat belts that it has a kind of creepiness factor to it.

Imagine that you get into a ridesharing car with your friends. You are sitting in swivel seats and having a good time, including drinking, which assuming you are legally able to drink, and since none of you is driving, you can readily go ahead and party in that AI self-driving car. Get lit, as they say. The AI at the start of the driving trip tells you all to put on your seat belts. You all comply.

During the driving journey, and perhaps after getting a bit tipsy, some of you decide to remove your seat belts. The AI is likely going to be able to detect this. The sensors in the seat belt will inform the AI. The inward facing cameras will be continually scanned by the AI and it will be able to visually detect that the seat belts have been removed. The AI speaks up and tells you all that it is important that you keep your seat belts intact.

Creepy? I guess so. If I say it's for your own protection, does that help?

Anyway, let's move past the privacy issues that this raises, which I've covered elsewhere, and focus again on the AI aspects and the use of the seat belts.

Suppose that in their drunken state, these passengers refuse to put back on their seat belts. Since this is a ridesharing car, if the self-driving car makes a sudden stop, doing so lawfully to save the passengers, but if the passengers than go flying around the interior, who is responsible? Is it the ridesharing service because they did not enforce the use of seat belts? Is it the miscreants that opted to refuse compliance with the AI urged use of the seat belts?

I am betting that a lawyer will be happy to go after the ridesharing service. All told, I'd guess that we'll eventually need to decide as a society what we want done about these kinds of situations. The easiest "solution" is that if the AI detects the seat belts are not being used, or being used improperly, and if the passengers won't comply, the AI would indicate it is bringing the ride to a gradual halt and will pull over to the side of the road.

This is not an entirely satisfactory solution, as you can imagine, because if the passengers are drunk, and suppose they then get out of the ridesharing car and get injured, because they were brought to a halt at the side of the road, who is to blame for that?

I'll remove the drunkenness from the equation, since I don't want you to get mired into thinking that's the only situation involving this kind of dilemma. You put your children into a Level 5 AI self-driving car and tell it to take them to school. When you got them into the AI self-driving car, they all dutifully put on their seat belts. Away the AI self-driving car goes.

Once it gets not even down the block, the kids all take off their seat belts. They want to roam around inside the AI self-driving car and have some fun. No stinking seat belts for them. The AI detects that the kids have removed their seat belts. It gives them a stern warning. They laugh and mock the AI. What now?

It could be that the AI tries to dial-up the parents and get them onto an interior display screen, showing them via the camera the crazed children playing around inside the AI self-driving car. I'm assuming those kids are going to be in deep trouble that night when they get back home. This "solution" might not be viable either due to the potential that the AI cannot reach the parents, perhaps due to electronic communications blockages or the parents are not available, etc.

You might say that the AI should just immediately turn around and take the rebelling children back to their home. This is not a good solution either because they are now presumably not wearing their seat belts, and for whatever distance the AI needs to drive back to the home, those kids are all in danger because they are not wearing their seat belts. Plus, it could be that the parent has already left the home and the AI would be taking those kinds back to an empty house anyway.

The whole topic about children being inside a Level 5 AI self-driving car without any adult supervision is one that we as a society have not yet broached.

There are lots of other issues that can arise and there is a slew of questions yet to be asked and resolved. I realize that you might insist that we don't let children ride alone in a Level 5 AI self-driving car, but I'd say that will either be a proposed law that no one will agree to, or a law that many will break. It is going to be very tempting to use the AI self-driving car as a means to transport your children to school, and to football practice, and to the dentist, and so on, doing so on your behalf and without having to have an adult present in the self-driving car.

I've predicted that this will likely lead to a new job or role in our society, namely being the position of an AI self-driving car ride-along adult that can supervise children that are in the AI self-driving car. It requires no driving ability and nor license to drive. It is in a sense a nanny-like role. I can envision ridesharing services that will try to differentiate themselves from other ridesharing services by providing these "in-car nanny services" for an added fee when you use their ridesharing Level 5 AI self-driving cars.

Conclusion

I remember when I was a child that my parents would sometimes turnaround from the front seat of the car and loudly tell me and my siblings that we better stop messing around or we'd be in a lot of trouble. That usually worked, and we settled down. At least for a few minutes.

For AI self-driving cars that are less than Level 5, the use of seat belts will still be crucial and amount to pretty much the same as today's conventional cars. There will likely though be human drivers and passengers that might become complacent when in a Level 3 and Level 4 self-driving car, and falsely believe they can either remove their seat belt or wiggle around it. The AI can likely detect this and act as a kind of seat belt cop.

When we get to the true Level 5 AI self-driving cars, the good news is that there is no longer a human driver that needs to be properly seat belted in. The bad news is that the passengers are bound to want to move around and have freedom within the moving car. Wearing a seat belt won't be the top of their list of things to do while in an AI self-driving car. Plus, with the variations in car interiors, the odds are that having conventional seat belts won't cut the mustard and we'll need other approaches to be invented or brought to the marketplace.

The toughest aspect about the true Level 5 AI self-driving cars involves having unattended children in the self-driving car. In theory, if an adult is present, you can hold the adult responsible for making sure that everyone on the self-driving car is properly wearing their seat belt at all times. Without an adult, what are we to do? The AI can certainly detect the tomfoolery, but it is not readily going to be able to enforce the seat belt policy per se.

There are lots of catchy sayings that have evolved around wearing seat belts. Click it or ticket. Confucius says wear your seat belt. No safety, know pain. Seat belts save lives, buckle up every time.

We'll need to come up with some news slogans for the advent of AI self-driving cars. AI says wear your seat belt. No seat belts, AI no go. The AI says, don't forget to fasten your seat belt. Well, I'm sure that someone can come up with something catchier than those potential tags. The real work is going to be solving the seat belt "problem" and leveraging the AI to aid in saving people by getting them to wear their seat belts. That's a worthy catchphrase.

CHAPTER 3
TINY EV'S
AND
AI SELF-DRIVING CARS

CHAPTER 3

TINY EV'S
AND
AI SELF-DRIVING CARS

Suppose you had available an Electrical Vehicle (EV) which was a small sized car that was incredibly inexpensive and could allow increased mobility for thousands or perhaps millions of people that otherwise did not have ready access to personal transportation? These so-called tiny-EV's are quickly gaining ground and especially so in China. Sometimes also referred to as micro-EV's or micro-cars, it is estimated that last year there were 1.75 million of them sold in China, which essentially doubles the number of conventional sized EV cars that were sold in China in that same year (an estimated 777,000).

There is a plethora of tiny-EV models and makers in China, numbering over 400 such auto makers. I realize that those familiar with this auto industry segment might carp about calling all of those manufacturers "auto makers" since the creation of tiny-EV's is not quite the picture of what we normally consider a true auto maker. Many of the firms making these tiny-EV's are nearly working out of a garage or auto parts boneyard. The tiny-EV's are at times outfitted with a garish array of parts and would generally fail most safety standards tests.

Speaking of safety, these tiny-EV's are often limited as to how fast they will go. The typical top range speed is around 25 to 45 miles per hour. This is presumably fast enough to get you readily to where you want to go, assuming shorter distance trips, and yet not so fast that it can get you into undue trouble. There are already various kinds of Low Speed EV's (LSEV) in the marketplace, perhaps you've seem them at golf courses, retirement home parks, and the like, though the LSEV's are usually more sturdily constructed and also intended for very limited driving environments and conditions.

One of the largest criticisms of the tiny-EV's is that they are made cheaply, and this includes tossing into the micro-car a lead-acid ultra-cheap battery. These no frills and dirt-cheap batteries are a potential toxic hazard. The booming growth of the tiny-EV's market is regrettably also creating a booming number of these ecologically damaging batteries. Some are worried that in the rush toward providing the tiny-EV's, a seemingly "good" thing for society, there is a pell-mell rush towards messing up the environment and causing some horrendous long-term health consequences.

Currently, in most jurisdictions in China, there is no requirement that the driver of a tiny-EV must have a driver's license. You could argue that this is okay since the micro-cars are, well, like driving an amusement park bumper car, and it doesn't take a rocket scientist to drive one. Others would say that it is a car, and as such, it ought to require having a driver's license. It's not simply have a piece of paper that concerns those that want the driver's license to be required, and instead that the drivers are many times ill-versed in driving.

You can obviously still do a lot of damage when driving a car that's topping out at 25 to 45 miles per hour. This "low speed" is still fast enough that you can readily hit and injure or kill a pedestrian. You could hit and injure or kill an animal that's on the roadway. You could crash into other tiny-EV's and create injuries or deaths. You could crash into full-sized cars and create injuries or deaths. You could smash into light posts, fire hydrants, and other property.

Overall, just because it is a tiny-EV does not mean that it cannot get involved in car collisions and nor that somehow those collisions will be injury-free or damage-free simply due to the lower top speeds involved.

While we're discussing collisions, let's also mention that the tiny-EV's are typically bereft of any substantive safety equipment and related doodads. The odds are that if you do get into an accident, there aren't any airbags to protect you, and the frame of the micro-car is marginally going to protect you. All told, you are pretty much driving a sardine can and anything that goes awry is going to potentially "fry" the sardine (that's the driver and possibly a squeezed-in passenger).

There is a mounting concern that people will choose to buy a tiny-EV even though they might have been able to afford a conventional full-sized car EV. At the cost of a tiny-EV, you could probably get several of them in comparison to getting one fuller sized EV. You can easily get a tiny-EV for everyone in your family, one for you, one for each of your offspring, one for your each of your relatives, and still have money left over. If this though what the public ought to be doing?

By encouraging the purchasing of the tiny-EV's, it is drawing away from the conventional EV market, which might lead to the demise or at least a delay of shifting us all toward full-sized EV's. Meanwhile, the tiny-EV's are increasing the roadway dangers for the drivers and the driving public. Yes, they are cheap and easy, but it could be a kind of invasion that we later on realize was a mistake to let happen. Tons of tiny-EV's and their toxic batteries, unlicensed drivers, high safety risks, and other downsides are not what everyone wants to see become prevalent on our roadways and certainly not become a dominant kind of EV. Indeed, there are some jurisdictions in China that have banned the sale and even the use of tiny-EV's on their roads.

On a jurisdictional matter, there is also a muddled indication of where you can drive the tiny-EV's. In some cities in China, you can drive them not only in the roadway with other full-sized cars, but you can also drive the tiny-EV's in the bicycle lanes.

Imagine that you are riding your bike in a bike lane and all of a sudden a "monstrous" tiny-EV zips up to you and nearly runs you off the road. This seems like a rather dangerous place for a tiny-EV to go. You can likely guess that the drivers of the tiny-EV's relish having legal access to use the bike lane. There you are in your tiny-EV, stuck in regular traffic and these behemoth regular-sized cars are all around you, and you suddenly dart into the bike lane to get ahead of the rest of the traffic.

I suppose it might almost feel like being surrounded by angry bees. If you are sitting in a regular car and waiting for the traffic ahead of you to start moving, it must be somewhat disconcerting to suddenly see these tiny-EV's racing down the bike lane and going past you. I'd bet too that the tiny-EV's then try to merge radically back into the regular traffic, particularly if the bike lane runs out or maybe is jammed with bicycle riders.

Let's consider how a regular sized car needs to cope with these angry bees. You already have your hands full trying to watch for other cars of a normal size. You likely also already watch for errant pedestrians and for meandering bicycle riders. Add to your list these tiny-EV's that can go relatively fast, meaning that at 25 to 45 miles per hour in city driving is pretty fast, and they can weave in and around the rest of the regular traffic. Can you even spot the tiny-EV that's ahead of you? What about the one behind you? What about the one coming alongside you and in your blind spot?

The typical price tag for a tiny-EV is about $1,000. If you were to insist that true safety features be included, it would undoubtedly jump up the price substantially. If you insisted that a driver's license was needed, it would likely decrease by far the number of drivers that might drive a tiny-EV. If you restricted the tiny-EV's to driving as regular cars must, meaning no more access to bike lanes, it would potentially dampen the traffic "busting" advantage of having a tiny-EV and it would become just another cog in the roadway snarl.

Essentially, making the tiny-EV's into being proper citizens of the driving world would imply they would no longer sell. The micro-car market as we know it would likely shrivel up and collapse. There are some though that argue it would force the "auto makers" to find some other more productive means to go after the market that is apparently eager to be served. Perhaps it might spur innovation to get the costs down for adding those required safety features and perhaps the roadways could be divided up into lanes for conventional car EV's and for the tiny-EV's.

Proponents of the tiny-EV's plead to not give up on them. Besides the convenience for short distance trips, and the claimed traffic reducing aspects (though having lots and lots of tiny-EV's can ultimately make traffic worse), these micro-cars are also easy to park into tight spots. You can potentially fit three tiny-EV's into the same space needed to park a regular sized car. This reduces in theory the amount of parking spaces needed and therefore the overall set aside for car parking in a tight city locale. One might argue that the physical space normally used to park regularly sized cars could then be repurposed to be a gentle grassy park or used in some other public benefiting way.

Not to be a party pooper, but there are those that contend the parking is actually worse off due to the tiny-EV's. The tiny-EV's are at times parked wherever the driver thinks they can get away with it. Park on the sidewalk, sure, if you can get away with it. Park in front of a fire hydrant, sure, do so if there's room available and if you think you won't get caught. There is also the concern that in the act of parking a tiny-EV, the driver can make rather reckless driving maneuvers. If you see a parking spot opening on the other side of the street, maybe just scoot your tiny-EV across the median, illegally, and do a quick U-turn in the roadway (illegal) and dive right into the vaunted spot.

In quick recap, there are hardly any standards regulating the tiny-EV's. The safety features are nearly nonexistent. The use of a toxic hazard battery is a grave concern. Letting them be driven in normal traffic and into the bike lane seems to setup dangerous driving and roadway conditions. Lack of requirements of a driver's license means that the drivers are presumably ill-prepared to properly drive the tiny-EV's. If the tiny-EV gets into an accident, it's bound to be an untoward result for the occupants and could cause some quite serious injury, damage, or death to other parties.

Those are many of the downsides about the tiny-EV's.

Let's consider the other side of the coin, the upsides. They are inexpensive and so affordable for the masses. They are limited in their top speeds so presumably more manageable on the roadways. The tiny-EV's allow for greater mobility and especially for those that normally might not have mobility options. Some would try to suggest they are like having a scooter, and yet more capable and perhaps even "safer" in comparison to using a scooter (of course, that's debatable).

Will the micro-cars grow in popularity? Many predict it definitely will. Is there a possibility of a shakeout due to the tiny-EV's getting into killer accidents and becoming roadway pests? Many predict there definitely will be. Might it be regulated out-of-business by wanting to do the "right thing" and make them safer and more sound? Some would say that could happen, while others argue that the "auto makers" might step-up and make improvements and yet still keep many of the advantages available.

What's your take on the tiny-EV's? Love them and keep them coming? Hate them and believe they should be relegated to the junk heap? Time will tell.

What does this have to do with AI self-driving cars?

At the Cybernetic AI Self-Driving Car Institute, we are developing AI software for self-driving cars. It is important to consider the impacts of tiny-EV's on the advent of AI self-driving cars.

Allow me to elaborate.

I'd like to first clarify and introduce the notion that there are varying levels of AI self-driving cars. The topmost level is considered Level 5. A Level 5 self-driving car is one that is being driven by the AI and there is no human driver involved. For the design of Level 5 self-driving cars, the auto makers are even removing the gas pedal, brake pedal, and steering wheel, since those are contraptions used by human drivers. The Level 5 self-driving car is not being driven by a human and nor is there an expectation that a human driver will be present in the self-driving car. It's all on the shoulders of the AI to drive the car.

For self-driving cars less than a Level 5, there must be a human driver present in the car. The human driver is currently considered the responsible party for the acts of the car. The AI and the human driver are co-sharing the driving task. In spite of this co-sharing, the human is supposed to remain fully immersed into the driving task and be ready at all times to perform the driving task. I've repeatedly warned about the dangers of this co-sharing arrangement and predicted it will produce many untoward results.

Let's focus herein on the true Level 5 self-driving car. Much of the comments apply to the less than Level 5 self-driving cars too, but the fully autonomous AI self-driving car will receive the most attention in this discussion.

Here's the usual steps involved in the AI driving task:

- Sensor data collection and interpretation
- Sensor fusion
- Virtual world model updating
- AI action planning
- Car controls command issuance

Another key aspect of AI self-driving cars is that they will be driving on our roadways in the midst of human driven cars too. There are some pundits of AI self-driving cars that continually refer to a utopian world in which there are only AI self-driving cars on the public roads. Currently there are about 250+ million conventional cars in the United States alone, and those cars are not going to magically disappear or become true Level 5 AI self-driving cars overnight.

Indeed, the use of human driven cars will last for many years, likely many decades, and the advent of AI self-driving cars will occur while there are still human driven cars on the roads. This is a crucial point since this means that the AI of self-driving cars needs to be able to contend with not just other AI self-driving cars, but also contend with human driven cars. It is easy to envision a simplistic and rather unrealistic world in which all AI self-driving cars are politely interacting with each other and being civil about roadway interactions. That's not what is going to be happening for the foreseeable future. AI self-driving cars and human driven cars will need to be able to cope with each other.

Returning to the topic of tiny-EV's, let's consider how the advent of AI self-driving cars might be impacted.

First, let's consider whether or not a tiny-EV might be outfitted as an AI self-driving car.

The odds of being able to make a tiny-EV into being a true Level 5 AI self-driving car is quite slim right now. At this time, the costs of the needed AI hardware and software would push the tiny-EV out of its cherished low-end pricing and instead shove the pricing way up into the stratosphere. You might as well buy a full-sized EV car if you are willing to incur the added cost for becoming an AI self-driving micro-car.

I've already stated in my writings and presentations that I am doubtful we'll be able to make conventional cars into AI self-driving cars via the use of any kind of aftermarket add-ons. Instead, the added AI hardware and software will need to be integrated into the self-driving car. I'm not saying that you cannot take a conventional car and make it into a true AI self-driving car. My emphasis is that the only likely way to do so is by having the auto maker and tech firm do this and not by simply selling a kit that you could go buy at your local auto parts store.

There are some that have been trying to sell such add-on kits. In my view, these kits are highly dangerous. They give the illusion that you are upgrading your car to become AI-like, but the reality is that you are merely turning your car into maybe a Level 2 or Level 3, and yet doing so in the worst of ways. These kits are generally something you would be wise to steer clear from using and for which absolutely they do not turn any car into a true Level 5 AI self-driving car.

I know that some of those kit makers and others will accuse me of favoring the "big guys" (the auto makers and tech firms) and that my remarks are harming the "little guys" (mom-and-pop startups that are bringing these kits to the marketplace). There are some that might suggest I am part of a grand conspiracy by the major auto makers and tech firms, involving trying to monopolize the AI self-driving car market and squeeze out the smaller firms that might have innovative approaches.

Let me absolutely state that I am not part of a grand conspiracy and nor am I being fooled or taken in mindlessly by some grand conspiratorial effort. Well, I guess you could say that of course I would make such a claim, even if I was part of a conspiracy. Anyway, right now, the kits are not sufficient, and I believe I am on firm ground in saying so. Maybe this will change far off in the future.

On a related note, I am actually a staunch and outspoken encourager of innovation in this space and have stated as such in my writings and presentations, along with welcoming startups into the AI self-driving car industry.

Besides the cost barrier, there is also the aspect about the size of the AI hardware that would need to go into and onto a tiny-EV.

Imagine trying to outfit a micro-car with the various radar devices, the ultrasonic sensors, the LIDAR's, the cameras, and the like. You need to also include the various high-speed processors and memory chips. You need to add the networking communications devices, which would allow for crucial electronic communications including OTA (Over-The-Air) updating and the V2V (vehicle-to-vehicle) communications. For full-size cars and EV's there is already some concern about the added weight, size, and impacts to the design and shape of the vehicle. For a tiny-EV, it would be many times more pronounced of an impact.

At this time, the size and weight of those devices would severely weigh down and bloat the tiny-EV. You'd almost have the tail wagging the dog, in the sense that the amount of added equipment for trying to make them into an AI self-driving car might end-up making the tiny-EV into an overweight paperweight and it could barely move along. Though the sensors and other devices are admittedly increasingly getting miniaturized, please don't expect this to happen in any miracle way such that in any near-term horizon they would be so small that they would be unnoticeably added to a tiny-EV.

I am not saying it might never happen. I don't want to be one of those prognosticators that later on gets quoted for saying something that at the time made sense but later on looked pretty foolish. For example, the famous quote in Popular Mechanics magazine in 1949 that computers will be unlikely to weigh less than 1 ½ tons (which was a typical weight of the vacuum tube era mainframes), or the Ken Olsen quote in 1977 that there would be no reason for anyone to want to have a computer in their home (this was during the heyday of the minicomputer, prior to the advent of the PC).

Sure, it is possible that sometime in the future the apparatus used today for crafting an AI self-driving car will be super-inexpensive and super-tiny. The AI-related hardware could be so small and so cheap to make that it could be on the tiny-EV's and the cost bump would be negligible and the weight difference marginal. The AI software might be fully open sourced and not cost a dime to use. Who knows? I certainly hope that comes to fruition.

I don't think you should hold your breath since it is going to be a long time from now.

Another twist might be to outfit the tiny-EV's with a minimalist set of added hardware for the self-driving car aspects and then perhaps have the rest of everything happening in the cloud.

With the emergence of 5G, perhaps you could have the AI primarily working in the cloud. The tiny-EV would have barebones on-board systems. Via OTA or some equivalent, the tiny-EV would be continually shoving data up to the cloud and the AI in the could would be pushing down the needed car controls commands.

I am doubtful again that this is something we'll see in the near future. The kind of guaranteed communications you would need is beyond today's approaches. Presumably, if the tiny-EV's on-board systems lost touch with the mothership system, even for a moment, it could spell disaster for the tiny-EV and its occupants and bystanders. For now, the crux of the AI self-driving car capabilities needs to be on-board of the self-driving car.

I realize you might ask what about edge computing, perhaps having computing capabilities at the side of the roadways and therefore more likely ensuring rapt communications. Yes, that's another possibility. This use of the nearby computing would have various other risks and concerns. Not that it cannot be undertaken, but only that it is a long way off in the future too, perhaps as far away as the notion of the super-inexpensive and super-small sensors and other on-board hardware that might someday emerge.

Another perspective might be a federated approach.

Suppose we have each of the tiny-EV's with a minimalist set of AI related hardware. Let's also assume that there will be other nearby AI self-driving cars. This seems a reasonable assumption once AI self-driving cars become relatively prevalent. Of course, at the start of the emergence, it would not be the case and therefore this proposed federated approach would seem unlikely or premature.

In any case, in the federated approach we divide up the chores of doing the self-driving among several self-driving cars. You essentially split-up the workload. Some might say this is somewhat akin to how blockchain and Distributed Ledger Technology (DLT) functions. You push around the computational aspects and exploit a distributed kind of AI approach.

During the driving effort, each of the tiny-EV's is sharing with other nearby tiny-EV's, and perhaps also sharing with normal sized cars that are using AI self-driving car technology. Any of the tiny-EV's requests another nearby AI self-driving car to aid in figuring out the local surroundings and what is taking place. Via the use of V2V, plus likely the use of V2I (vehicle-to-infrastructure) electronic communications, it is conceivable that each of the AI's can help the other out.

This would be quite tricky and would need to include balancing the workloads. None of the requesters for assistance can end-up in a starvation mode. Furthermore, there is a chance that the other AI's get themselves into a swamped mode and are too overloaded. But, this is something of active research and the use of AI swarms is predicted to eventually become an essential aspect of overall AI systems deployments.

I'll repeat my earlier point that tiny-EV's in the near-term have little or no chance of becoming true Level 5 AI self-driving cars. For all the reasons I've already mentioned, it won't be happening any time soon, if ever.

That's not though the only angle related to AI self-driving cars.

Here's another perspective to consider, namely, how will AI self-driving cars cope with the tiny-EV's? Assume for now that the tiny-EV's are exactly as already stated in terms of being relatively unsafe and driven in a rather wild manner by unlicensed drivers.

I had already pointed out that a human driver of a normal sized car must find these "angry bees" quite a handful to deal with. Where is that darned tiny-EV? Is it behind me, in front of me, or maybe barreling along in the bike lane and I cannot yet see it or otherwise detect it?

We need to ask the same kinds of questions about an AI self-driving car of a normal size. Will the sensors be able to detect this zipping along tiny-EV's? Is the AI able to deal with having them as they rapidly and with a lowered profile enter into and out of traffic wherever they seem to want to do so?

It is already tough enough for the AI sensors to detect conventional sized cars. I realize you might say that is the sensors can detect a scooter or a motorcycle or a bike rider, shouldn't it be able to detect the tiny-EV's? I'd say what makes the tiny-EV an added twist is the speed factor, namely that it can go 25 to 45 miles per hour, which is likely faster than most scooters and most bike riders. In that manner, the tiny-EV is more like the maneuverability and speed of a motorcycle.

I think we can say that the AI should be able to much of the time detect the tiny-EV's, but without having augmented the sensors, the sensor fusion, the virtual model updating, and the rest of the AI system to deal with tiny-EV's, I would suggest that an AI self-driving car would not be as fully prepared.

It will be important to directly and intentionally build into the AI system the capabilities of dealing with the tiny-EV's. If you leave the AI to do whatever it already can do about other forms of mobile transport, I'd say there are chances of gaps or holes in what the AI ought to be doing about tiny-EV's.

Conclusion

Tiny-EV's. Sounds kind of quaint. They aren't quaint per se. They are on the roadways. They present a potential danger to their occupants and bystanders. They are cars but ones without the basics of safety and furthermore vehicles that can inadvertently encourage drivers to do rather wild kinds of driving. Coupled with allowing the tiny-EV to use bike lanes, it is a potential recipe for disastrous results on the roads.

That being said, it is a societal question as to whether or not the risks/rewards are appropriate. If we were to try and boost the safety and other facets of the tiny-EV, it would no longer have the mass appeal and affordability that it does today.

We are very unlikely to see any true AI self-driving car tiny-EV's in the foreseeable future due to the burden of cost and size that would make the tiny-EV no longer viable. The faraway future might prove otherwise due to the ongoing and unrelenting efforts to make AI systems less expensive and smaller in size.

Meanwhile, the AI systems being devised for true Level 5 AI self-driving cars need to make sure they incorporate the nuances of the tiny-EV's in terms of their smaller size, their agility of slipping around in traffic, their potential wildness in terms of how they are being driven, and so on.

There is already a lot that we expect a proficient and true AI self-driving car to be able to do, so let's make sure that we don't neglect those tiny-EV's. Angry bees are something not to be ignored. The AI system must have a bit of sufficient beekeeping to contend with and live in harmony with them, those tiny but powerful micro-car EV's.

CHAPTER 4
EMPATHETIC COMPUTING AND AI SELF-DRIVING CARS

CHAPTER 4

EMPATHETIC COMPUTING
AND AI SELF-DRIVING CARS

A friend of mine in college was known for being very stoic. You could tell him that you had broken your leg skiing and he'd show no emotion. He'd just sit there and stare at you. No words came forth. No expression on his face. You might tell him that your dog got run over, and he'd continue to be without any kind of emotional response. I believe that if you told him that <u>his</u> dog got run over, he'd have the same kind of non-reaction, though I suppose he might be curious enough to ask how it happened.

Some of us thought that he had watched way too many Star Trek TV shows and movies. He had become our version of Mr. Spock, the fictional character that generally showed little or no emotion.

In case, you've been living in a cave and aren't familiar with Star Trek, Spock was the science officer and first officer. To some degree, it was implied that his linage of Vulcan heritage allowed him through training and DNA to remain impartial and detached, shedding any emotion, though this was not entirely the case and he had mixed-blood with a human mother that "did him in" in terms of having to fight back at emotions bursting forth. At times, in some of the stories, he did show emotion, typically briefly and with a muted indication of it.

I'd like to remind that Spock was a character in a plot and not an actual person. We tried to emphasize this crucial aspect to our friend. Our friend seemed to believe that Spock was real or that even if not so, somehow it was possible to be like Spock. I knew my friend's parents and I assure they were not Vulcan, neither of them were. He therefore was already one step behind being so unemotional, presumably because wasn't already cooked into his DNA, as Spock's was.

Our friend eventually had a girlfriend. We assumed that he'd come out of his non-emotion impenetrable barrier bubble and certainly be at least emotional with regard to his girlfriend. No dice. At first, we assumed he was keeping up the pretense only with us, his male friends, and undoubtedly, he was emotional when behind-the-scenes with his girlfriend. A macho kind of thing. Whenever he insisted that he was acting toward us in the same manner as he acted toward his girlfriend, we simply nodded our heads as though we agreed to this obviously preposterous claim.

Turns out that his girlfriend confided in me that he was indeed a cold calculating machine and seemed to not express any emotions. He was this way all the time, according to her reports. For example, they had gone one time to a great sorority party and she was having a wonderful time, meanwhile he barely smiled and acted nonplused. They had gone hiking in the mountains and nearly fell from a cliff, yet he remained unnerved and cool as a cucumber. She assumed that eventually he'd come "out of his shell" if she just kept dating him (I believe it almost became an attractor as a type of challenge!).

Maybe he really was an early version of Mr. Spock? Note that the original Star Trek series took place probably around the year 2200 or so, and perhaps my friend became the basis for the future Mr. Spock. It's a time travel deal.

Anyway, I'd wager that most of us do express our emotions. Furthermore, we express our emotions at times as a response to someone else. The other person might tell us something in an unemotional way, and you might respond in an emotional way. Or, the other person might tell you something in an emotional way, and you might respond in an emotional way.

Thus, it can be that emotion begets emotion, stoking it from another person. That doesn't have to be the case and you can be conversing with someone on a seemingly unemotional basis and then opt to suddenly become emotional. There doesn't necessarily need to be a trigger by the other person. Nor does it necessarily need to be a tit-for-tat.

That being said, usually when a person is emotional toward you, the odds are they will likely be expecting an emotional laden response in return. When my friend was told about a mutual close friend that had broken their leg skiing and told so by someone that was crying and quite upset about the pain and suffering involved, it would likely be anticipated that the response would be one of great concern, sadness, and a flurry of aligned emotional evocations from him.

A lack of an emotional response in the leg broken instance would tend to signal that he didn't care about the other person. He didn't care that the other person had suffered an injury. What kind of a friend is that? How could he be so careless and without sympathy?

When you asked him about these kinds of matters, he would contend that by remaining unemotional, it gave him an added edge in life. He kept his head calm and collected. It would do little good for him to get cloudy and hazed by being emotional. For the friend that had broken a leg, the main logical aspect would be whether there is anything he could do to aid that person. Expressing emotion about it was wasted energy and effort and distracted by considering the logic of the matter.

Sure, that's what Mr. Spock would say. Watch any episode.

You might be familiar with the words of the famous holistic theorist Alfred Adler, a psychiatrist and philosopher that lived in the late 1800s and the early 1900s, in which he said that we should see with the eyes of another, hear with the ears of another, and feel with the heart of another.

73

The first two elements, the eyes and the ears, presumably can be done without any emotional attachment involved, if you consider the eyes as merely a collector of visual images and the ears as collectors of abstract sounds and noises. The third element, involving the heart, and the accompanying aspects of feelings, pushes us squarely into the realm of emotions.

Of course, I don't believe that Adler was suggesting that the eyes and ears are devoid of emotion, and rather the opposite that you can best gain a sense of another person by experiencing the emotion that they express and inures by what they see, and by what they hear, along with matters of the heart.

I bring up Adler's quote because there are many that assert you cannot really understand and be aligned with another person if you don't walk in their emotional shoes.

You don't necessarily need to exhibit the same exact emotions, but you ought to at least have some emotions that come forth and be able to understand and comprehend their emotions. If the other person is crying in despair, it does not mean you can only respond by crying in despair too. Instead, perhaps you break out into a wild laughter and this might spark the other person out of their despair and join you in the laugher. It's not a simple mating of one emotion echoed by the same emotion in the other.

Let's then postulate a simple model about emotion.

One aspect is the ability to detect emotion of others.

The other aspect is for you to emit emotion.

So, you are talking with someone, and you detect their emotion, and you might then respond with emotion. As mentioned before, it is not necessarily the case that you would always do the detection and a corresponding emission of emotion. It is more complex than that.

For example, we all wondered whether my friend was perhaps detecting emotion and then storing up his own emotion. If that was the case, we wondered what would happen one day if suddenly all of that pent-up emotion was unleashed, all at once. A cavalcade of emotion might emerge. A tsunami of emotion. A bursting dam of emotion.

Being empathetic is considered a capability of being able to exhibit a high degree of understanding about other people's emotions, both their exhibited and hidden emotions. Per Adler, this implies that you need to be like a sponge and soak in the other person's emotions. Only once you've gotten immersed in those emotions, only then can you truly be empathetic or an empath, some would say.

Can you be empathetic without also exhibiting emotion? In other words, can you do a tremendous job of detecting the emotion of others, and yet be like my friend in terms of never emitting emotions yourself?

That's an age-old question and takes us down a bit of a rabbit hole. Some claim that if you don't emit emotion, you can never prove that you felt the emotion of another, and nor can you then get on the same plain or mental emotional level as the other. I assure you my friend would say that's hogwash and he separated (or thought he did) the ability of emotion recognition versus the personal embodiment of emotion.

One danger that some suggest can occur if you are emitting emotion is that you might get caught up in an emotion contagion. That's when you detect the emotion of another and in an almost autonomic way you immediately exhibit that same emotion. You can see this sometimes in action. Suppose you have a room of close friends and one suddenly starts crying, others can also start to cry, even though maybe they don't exactly know why the other people are crying. It becomes an infectious emotion. Crying can be like that. Laughing can be like that.

I recall a joke that was told one time while I was on a hike with the Boy Scouts (I was an Assistant Scout Master at the time). We had been hiking for miles upon miles. The day was long. We were exhausted and looking forward to reaching camp. One of the younger Scouts told a joke about a turtle and a hare, for which I don't remember the details as it was utterly without any sense and a completely jumbled-up joke. Though at first, I was trying to figure out the nature of the joke, and hoped that I could "repair" the joke into whatever it was supposed to be, suddenly an older Scout nearby started laughing.

Then, another Scout started laughing. Then another. And so on. We were stretched out on this hike over a distance of maybe a football field size line, each Scout trudging along and following the footsteps of the Scout ahead of them. Within moments, every single Scout and all of the adult Scout leaders were all laughing. It was an amazing sight to see.

Later on, at the evening campfire, I asked the other adult Scout leaders if they could make sense of the botched joke. I had assumed that they had heard the joke and either already knew what the young Scout was attempting to say, or found it funny because it was perhaps an entirely nonsensical joke. Well, none of them had heard the actual joke. They were too far away. They had laughed because everyone else was laughing, and partially I'd guess due to the exhaustion of the hike. It was an infectious spread of laughter.

Sometimes when you exhibit emotion it can come across as a form of pity. This might not be what you intended. I knew an adult volunteer that aided us with the Scouts and every time a Scout said they had been either physically hurt during a hike or even mentally anguished, this adult responded with laughter. It was kind of weird at first. The reaction by the Scout telling about their hardship was to recoil from this response. It seemed like the adult was mocking the Scout or maybe trying to show a sense of feeling sorry for them, but it didn't come across very well.

There is ongoing research trying to figure out how the brain incorporates emotions. Can we somehow separate out a portion of the brain that is solely about emotions and parse it away from the logical side of the brain? Or, are emotions and logic interwoven in the neurons and neuronal connections such that they are not separable. In spite of Adler's indication about the heart, modern day science would say the physical heart has nothing to do with emotions and it's all in your head. The brain and its currently unknown manner of how it exactly functions is nonetheless the engine that manifests emotion for us.

Sometimes empathy is coupled with the word affective. This is usually done to clarify that the type of empathy has to do with emotions, since presumably you could have other kinds of empathy. For example, some assert that cognitive empathy is being able to detect another person's mental state, which might or might not be infused with emotion. Herein, I'm going to refer to empathy as affective empathy, which I am intending to suggest is emotional empathy, namely empathy shaped around emotions.

I've previously written and spoken about emotion recognition in the context of computers that are programmed to be able to detect the emotion of humans. This is a budding area of Artificial Intelligence (AI). I'm going to augment my prior discussions about emotion recognition by now including the emitting of emotions.

Recall that I earlier herein had said that we should consider the emotional empathy or now I'll say affective empathy as consisting of two distinct constructs, the act of emotion recognition, and the act of emotion emission.

I want to mainly explore the emotion emission aspects herein. The notion is that we might want to build AI that can recognize emotion, along with being able to exhibit emotion. That's right, I'm suggesting that the AI would emit emotion.

This seems contrary to what we consider AI to be. Most people would assert that AI is supposed to be like Mr. Spock, or more properly another fictional character in the Star Trek series known as Data. Data was a robot of a futuristic nature that was continually trying to grasp what human emotions are all about and craved that someday "it" would have emotions too.

There might be some handy reasons to have the AI exhibit emotion, which I'll be covering shortly. First, let's do a quick look at what do we mean by the notion of emotions.

When referring to emotions, there are lots of varied definitions of what kinds of emotions exist. Some try to say that similar to how colors have a base set and you can then mix-and-match those base colors to render additional colors, so the same applies to emotions. They assert that there are some fundamental emotions and we then mix-and-match those to get other emotions. But, there is much disagreement about what are the core or fundamental emotions and it's generally an unsettled debate.

One viewpoint has been that there are six core emotions:

- Anger
- Disgust
- Fear
- Happiness
- Sadness
- Surprise

I'm guessing that if you closely consider those six, you'll maybe right away start to question how those six are the core. Aren't there other emotions that could also be considered core? How would those six be combined to make all of the other seemingly emotions that we have? And so on. This highlights my point about there being quite a debate on this matter.

Some claim that these emotions are also to be considered core:

- Amusement
- Awe
- Contentment
- Desire
- Embarrassment
- Pain
- Relief
- Sympathy

Some further claim these are also considered core:

- Boredom
- Confusion
- Interest
- Pride
- Shame
- Contempt
- Interest
- Relief
- Triumph

For purposes herein, we'll go ahead and assume that any of those aforementioned emotions are fair game as emotional states. There's no need to belabor the point just now.

Affective empathetic computing or also known as affective empathetic AI is the aspect of trying to get a machine to recognize emotions in others, which has been the mainstay so far, and we ought to also add that it includes the emission of emotions by the machine.

That last addition is a bit controversial.

The first part, recognizing the emotions of others, seems to have a clear-cut use case. If the AI can figure out that you are crying, for example, it might be able to adjust whatever interaction you are having with the AI to take into account that you are indeed crying.

Suppose you are crying hysterically. This likely implies that no matter what the AI system might be saying to you, some or maybe even none of what you are being told might register with you. You could be so emotionally overwhelmed that you aren't making any sense of what the AI is telling you. I'm sure you've seen people that get themselves caught up in a crying fit, and it often is impossible to try and ferret out why, and nor get them into a useful conversation.

I remember one young Scout that came running up to me and he was crying uncontrollably. I was worried that he was physically hurt in some non-apparent manner (I looked of course to see whether he was bleeding or maybe had a wound or had any other obvious signs of something broken). I asked him what was wrong. He kept crying. I urged him to use his words. He kept crying. I told him that I had no idea why he was crying and that for me to help him, I needed him to either point at what was wrong or show me what was wrong or tell me what was wrong. Something, anything, more so than crying.

He kept crying. This now was getting me distressed since he was essentially incommunicado. The crying was rather worrisome. Uncontrollably crying could mean that he might be entering into shock. I got down on one knee, looked him straight in the eye, reached out and held him with my arms, and in a soothing and direct voice, I asked him to tell me his name. He blurted out his name. We were now getting somewhere. Anyway, the end of the story was that he had seen another Scout get cut by a pocket knife and there had been blood, and it had spooked him to no end. Everyone it turns out was okay, after the dust settled on the matter.

The point of the story is that the Scout was so consumed by emotion that no matter what I was saying seemed to register with him.

That's why it would be handy for AI to be able to recognize emotion in humans. Doing so would allow the AI to be able to adjust whatever actions or efforts the AI is doing, based on the perceived emotional state of the human. Maybe the AI would be better off not trying to offer logical explanation to someone hysterically crying and wait until the crying subsides. Or, maybe take another tact, such as my example of asking the person's name, shifting attention away from whatever the matter is at hand, and instead helping the person onto more familiar and less emotional ground.

What does this have to do with AI self-driving cars?

At the Cybernetic AI Self-Driving Car Institute, we are developing AI software for self-driving cars. The use of emotional recognition for AI self-driving cars is an emerging area of interest and will likely be crucial for interactions between the AI and human drivers and passengers (and others). I would also assert that affective empathetic AI or computing involving emotional emissions is vital too.

Allow me to elaborate.

I'd like to first clarify and introduce the notion that there are varying levels of AI self-driving cars. The topmost level is considered Level 5. A Level 5 self-driving car is one that is being driven by the AI and there is no human driver involved. For the design of Level 5 self-driving cars, the auto makers are even removing the gas pedal, brake pedal, and steering wheel, since those are contraptions used by human drivers. The Level 5 self-driving car is not being driven by a human and nor is there an expectation that a human driver will be present in the self-driving car. It's all on the shoulders of the AI to drive the car.

For self-driving cars less than a Level 5, there must be a human driver present in the car. The human driver is currently considered the responsible party for the acts of the car. The AI and the human driver are co-sharing the driving task. In spite of this co-sharing, the human is supposed to remain fully immersed into the driving task and be ready at all times to perform the driving task. I've repeatedly warned about the dangers of this co-sharing arrangement and predicted it will produce many untoward results.

Let's focus herein on the true Level 5 self-driving car. Much of the comments apply to the less than Level 5 self-driving cars too, but the fully autonomous AI self-driving car will receive the most attention in this discussion.

Here's the usual steps involved in the AI driving task:

- Sensor data collection and interpretation
- Sensor fusion
- Virtual world model updating
- AI action planning
- Car controls command issuance

Another key aspect of AI self-driving cars is that they will be driving on our roadways in the midst of human driven cars too. There are some pundits of AI self-driving cars that continually refer to a utopian world in which there are only AI self-driving cars on the public roads. Currently there are about 250+ million conventional cars in the United States alone, and those cars are not going to magically disappear or become true Level 5 AI self-driving cars overnight.

Indeed, the use of human driven cars will last for many years, likely many decades, and the advent of AI self-driving cars will occur while there are still human driven cars on the roads. This is a crucial point since this means that the AI of self-driving cars needs to be able to contend with not just other AI self-driving cars, but also contend with human driven cars.

It is easy to envision a simplistic and rather unrealistic world in which all AI self-driving cars are politely interacting with each other and being civil about roadway interactions. That's not what is going to be happening for the foreseeable future. AI self-driving cars and human driven cars will need to be able to cope with each other.

Returning to the topic of affective empathetic computing or AI, I'm going to primarily focus on emotions emissions and less so on emotional recognition herein.

Let's assume that we've been able to get an AI system to do a pretty good job of detecting emotions of others. This is not so easy, and I don't want to imply it is. Nonetheless, I'd bet it is something that we'll gradually be able to do a better and better job of having the AI do.

Should the AI also exhibit emotion?

As already mentioned, some believe that the AI should be like Mr. Spock or Data and never exhibit emotion. Like they say, it should be just the facts, and only the facts, all of the time.

One good reason to not have the AI showcase emotion is because "it doesn't mean it." Some would argue that it is a false front to have AI seem to cry, or laugh, or get angry, and so on. There is no there, there, in the sense that it's not as though the AI is indeed actually happy or sad. The emission of emotions would be no different than the AI emitting the numbers 1, 2, and 3. It is simply programmed in a manner to exhibit what we humans consider to be emotions.

Emotions emission would be a con. It would be a scam.

Besides the criticism that the AI doesn't mean it, there is also the concern that it implies to the person receiving the emotion emission that the AI does mean it. This falsely adds to the anthropomorphizing of the AI. If a person begins to believe that the AI is "real" in terms of having human-like characteristics, the person might ascribe abilities to the AI that it doesn't have. This could get the person into a dire state since they are making assumptions that could backfire.

Suppose a human is a passenger in a true Level 5 AI self-driving car. The person is giving commands to the AI system as to where the person wants to be driven. Rather than simplistic one-word commands, let's assume the AI is using a more fluent and fluid Natural Language Processing (NLP) capability. This allows some dialogue with the human occupant, akin to what a Siri or Alexa might do, though we soon will have much greater NLP than the stuff we experience today.

The person says that they've had a rough day. Troubles at work. Troubles at home. Troubles everywhere. In terms of where to drive, the person tells the AI that it might as well drive him to the pier and drive off the edge of it.

What should the AI do?

If this was a ridesharing service and the driver was a human, what would the human driver do?

I doubt that the human driver would dutifully start the engine and drive to the end of the pier. Presumably, the human driver would at least ignore the suggestion or request. Better still, there might be some affective empathy expressed. The driver, sensing the distraught emotional state of the passenger, might offer a shoulder to cry on (not literally!), and engage in a dialogue about how bad the person's day is and whether there is someplace to drive the person that might cheer them up.

It's conceivable that the human driver might try to lighten the mood. Maybe the human driver tells the passenger that life is worth living for. He might tell the passenger that in his own life, he'd had some really down periods, and in fact his parents just recently passed away. The driver and the passenger now commiserate together. The passenger begins to tear up. The driver begins to tear up. They share a moment of togetherness, both of them reflecting on the unfairness of life.

Is that what the AI should do?

I realize you can quibble with my story about the human driver and point out that there are a myriad of ways in which the human driver might respond to the passenger. I admit that, but I'd also like to point out that my scenario is pretty realistic. I know this because I had a ridesharing driver tell me a similar story the other day about the passenger that had just been in his car, before I got into his car. I believe the story he told me to be true and it certainly seems reasonably realistic.

Back to my question, would we want the AI to do the same thing that the human driver did?

This would consist of the AI attempting to be affectively empathetic and besides detecting the state of emotion of the passenger, also emitting emotion as paired up for the situation. In this case, the

AI would presumably "cry" or do the equivalent of whatever we've setup the AI to showcase, creating that moment of bonding that the human driver had done with the distraught passenger.

As an aside, if you are wondering how would the AI of a self-driving car do the equivalent of "crying," which it is not going to be a robotic head and body sitting in the driver's seat (quite unlikely) and nor have liquid tear ducts embedded into the robotic head, the easy answer is that we might have a screen displaying a cartoonish mouth and eyes, shown on an LED display inside the AI self-driving car. The crying could consist of the cartoonish face having animated tear drops that go down the face.

You might debate whether that is the same as a human driver that has tears, and maybe it isn't in the sense that the passenger might not be heart struck by the animated crying, but there is ongoing research that suggests that people do indeed react emotionally to such simple animated renderings.

The overarching theme is that the AI is emitting emotions.

I've used this example of crying, but we could have the AI appear to be laughing, or appear to be angry, or appear to have any of a number of emotions. I'm sure too that with added research, we'll be able to get better and better at how to "best" display these emotions, attempting to get as realistic a response as feasible.

Some people would say this is outrageous and a complete distortion of human emotions. It undercuts the truthfulness of emotions, they would say. I don't want to burst that bubble, but I would like to point out that actors do this same thing every day. Aren't they "artificially" creating emotions to try and get us to respond? Seems to me that's part of their normal job description.

Does an actor up on the big screen that is crying during a tender scene in the movie have to be actually experiencing that emotion and doing so as a real element of life? Or, can they be putting on the emotion as a pretend? I ask you how you would even know the difference. A really good actor can look utterly sincere in their crying or laughing or anger, and you would assume they must be "experiencing" it, and yet when you ask them how they did it, they might say that's what they do.

Here's something that will get your goat, if you are in the camp about the sincerity and sanctity of emotions. I nearly hesitate to tell you.

When I talked with the ridesharing driver and he told me the story of what had just happened in his car, I offered my concern on his behalf about the bad turns in his life and the recent loss of his parents. He seemed slightly taken aback. He told me that his parents had passed away years ago. What, I asked? Yep, he told me that he had said that it was recent in hopes of being more empathetic with the passenger. When I mildly questioned the ethics of that approach, he insisted that it was all true that his parents were no longer alive, and the part about the timing was inconsequential to the significance of the matter.

If we are willing to put aside for the moment the aspect that the AI doesn't mean it when it emits emotion, and if we agree that the emitting of emotion can potentially create a greater bond with a human, and if the bonding can aid the human, would we then be okay in terms of emitting the emotions?

This certainly takes us onto ethical matters about the nature of mankind and machines. For AI self-driving cars in particular, are we willing as a society to have the AI "pretend" to get emotional, assuming that it is being done for the betterment of mankind. Of course, there is going to be quite a debate about how we'll be able to judge that the AI emotions emissions are indeed for the betterment of humans.

Let's pretend that the AI did the same thing as the human driver and appeared to cry a tear with the passenger. Suppose this becomes a man-machine bonding moment. The passenger has found a friend. Maybe the AI then prods the passenger to consider driving to a bar that's about a half hour drive away and suggests that the passenger would likely get into a happier mood at the bar. What a great and friendly suggestion. Nice!

Meanwhile, suppose unbeknownst to the passenger, the bar has already established a deal with the ridesharing firm and paid the ridesharing firm to try and get people to go there. The ridesharing service runs ads about the bar and whenever possible attempts to get passengers to visit that particular bar. Plus, the ridesharing company makes more money for longer trips, and though there's a bar just two blocks away, this bar is a hefty trip of a half hour away and will be a better money-making trip.

Ouch! Did the AI emotion emission make the passenger feel better, and if so, what about the motives for doing so, along with the rather self-serving "manipulation" of the human passenger for the gain of the ridesharing firm.

We're going to have a difficult time trying to discern when the affective empathetic AI is for "good" versus for other purposes (I'm sure the ridesharing firm would say that it was for the good, since it was better for the passenger to go to a known bar than a randomly chosen one two blocks away!).

Some would say that the affective empathetic AI could be a tremendous boon to the mental health of our society. If people are going to be riding in true Level 5 AI self-driving cars and perhaps doing a lot more traveling via cars because of the AI advances, this means that us humans will have lots of dedicated time with our AI of our AI self-driving cars.

Right now, I commute to work each morning and afternoon, spending around three to maybe four hours a day in my car. I watch the traffic around me. I listen to the news on the radio. I make some phone calls. I while away the time by blending my driving efforts with doing things that hopefully don't distract from the driving, and yet help overcome the tedium of the driving. Plus, these other activities make me additionally productive in those otherwise mundane several hours, or at least enrich me beyond just driving my car.

When I commute to work in a true Level 5 AI self-driving car, I will then have those three to four hours for whatever purpose I'd like to use them. I am not driving the car. The AI is driving the car. I might take a snooze and sleep in the self-driving car as it is whisking me to work or from work. I might watch videos that are streamed into my self-driving car. And so on.

Suppose that the AI of my self-driving car opted to try and interact with me, doing so beyond the sole purpose of getting an indication of where I wanted to have the AI drive the self-driving car. Using its emotion recognition, it detects whether I'm doing okay and headed to work in a happy mood or not. Maybe on this day I seem to be upset and concerned. What's going on, the AI asks me?

I mention that I was playing poker at a friend's house last night and lost $500 at the table. I was going to use that money for other purposes. Darn it, I should not have kept betting on the game. The AI interprets this and responds with a variation of Alfred Lord Tennyson's famous quote, it is better to have played and lost than to never have played at all. The AI then offers a short chortle of laugher. It gets me into a good mood and I laugh too.

Over time, the AI is collecting my emotional states. These aspects are routinely being uploaded to the cloud, via the Over-The-Air (OTA) electronic capability of the self-driving car and with a connection to the auto maker or tech firm that made the system.

Turns out that I nearly always play poker on Monday nights and I seem to nearly always lose, and on Tuesday mornings I'm usually in a bad mood. The AI gradually catches onto this pattern, using a variant of Machine Learning and Deep Learning in analyzing the collected data of the interactions with me while I am in the AI self-driving car. This allows the AI to greet me on Tuesday mornings by personalizing the greeting, mentioning that hopefully I came out ahead at the table last night.

The AI of your self-driving car could eventually "know" you better than other humans might know you, in the sense that with the vast amount of time you are spending inside the AI self-driving car, doing many journeys and more than you would as a driver, and with the AI collecting the data and interpreting it. This data includes the emotion recognition aspects and the emotion emission aspects.

Creepy? Scary? Maybe so. There is nothing about this that is beyond the expectation of where AI is heading. Notice that I am not suggesting that the AI is sentient. Nope. I am not going to get bogged down in that one. For those of you that might try to argue that the AI as I have described it would need to sentient, I don't think so. What I have described could be done with pretty much today's capability of AI.

Conclusion

Affective empathetic AI is a combination of emotion recognition and emotion emissions. Some say that we should skip the emotion emissions part of things. It's bad, real bad. Others would say that if we are going to have AI systems interacting with humans, it will be important to interact in a manner that humans are most accustomed to, which includes that other beings have emotions (in this case, the AI, though I am not suggesting it is a "being" in any living manner).

I've not said much about how the AI is going to deliberate about emotions. The emotion recognition involves seeing a person and hearing a person, and then gauging their emotional state. Like I said about Adler, there is more to emotion detection than a merely visual images and sounds. The AI will need to interpret the images and sounds, using those in a programmed way or via some kind of Machine Learned manner to interpret them and ascertain what to next do.

Similarly, the AI needs to calculate when to best emit emotions. If it does so randomly, the human would certainly catch onto the "pretend" nature of the emotions. You could even say that if the AI offers emotion emissions of the wrong kind at the wrong time, it might enrage the human. Probably not the right way to proceed, though there are certainly circumstances wherein humans purposely desire to have someone else get enraged.

What about Adler's indication that you need to get into the heart of the other person. That's murky from an AI perspective. The question is whether or not the AI can skip the heart part and still come across as a seemingly emotionally astute entity that also expresses emotion.

I think that's a pretty easy challenge, far less so than an intellect challenge of being able to exhibit intelligence (aka Turing Test). My answer is that yes, the AI will be able to convince people that it "understands" their emotion and that it appears to also experience and emit emotion. Maybe not all of the people, and maybe not all of the time, but for a lot of the time and for a lot of the people.

I've altered Lincoln's famous saying and omitted the word "fool" in terms of fooling people. Is the AI, which was developed by humans, which I mention so that you won't believe that the AI just somehow concocted things on its own, is this human devised AI fooling people? And if so, is it wrong and should be banned? Or is it a good thing and will be a boon. Time will tell. Or maybe we should ask the affective empathetic AI and see what is says and does.

CHAPTER 5

ETHICS GLOBAL VARIATIONS AND AI SELF-DRIVING CARS

CHAPTER 5

ETHICS GLOBAL

VARIATIONS

AND

AI SELF-DRIVING CARS

We are not all the same. In Brazil, they eat winged queen ants that they fry or dip into chocolate. In Ghana, they eat termites in rural areas, which provide proteins, fats, and oils into their diets. Thailand is known for munching on grasshoppers and crickets, doing so in the same manner that Americans might snack on nuts and potato chips. Generally, things that people are eating in one part of the world can be considered icky in another part of the world. Your sensibilities about what is okay to eat and what is verboten or repulsive to eat is greatly shaped by your cultural norms.

Let's agree then that there are international differences among peoples. There is no single food-eating code that the entire world has reached an agreement to abide with. Is it wrong to eat termites or ants, in the sense that if your cultural norm is to not eat those creatures, must it be "wrong" for other peoples to do so? You might sneer at such eating habits, and yet if you are routinely eating chicken or burgers, why isn't it equally permissible for others to look down upon your choice of food. Perhaps they might consider those chicken sandwiches you devour to be outlandish, outrageous, and out-of-sorts.

You might say that we are making ethical or moral decisions about what we believe is proper to eat and what is not proper to eat. One dimension of this ethical or moral judgment is based on what your cultural norm consists of. Another dimension could be to try and include a scientific basis such as asserting that one type of item has more dietary advantages over another. There is an economic dimension too, since it could be that the economically viable choices are based on what resources exist near to the people that consume the items and so they are choosing to eat that which has the lower cost to obtain.

Eating is actually serious business. The will and strength of the people can greatly depend upon their stomachs. There are many people in the world that do not get enough food, or they get food that is insufficient for sustainable long-term health. It is easy to take food for granted in some parts of the world where it is relatively plentiful and affordable. Food is a basic sustenance of life. You could say that it has life-or-death consequences, though it can be hard to see that aspect on a day-to-day basis and it is not necessarily obvious to the eye unless you are among those that do not have food or have inadequate kinds of food.

I bring up the ethical underpinnings about food to help bring attention to something else that also involves ethical and moral elements, but for which at first glance it might not seem to do so.

Automated systems and the emergence of widespread applications of Artificial Intelligence (AI) are also laden with ethical and moral conundrums.

For most AI developers, they are likely steeped in the technology of trying to craft AI applications, for which the ethical and moral elements are not quite so apparent to them. When you are challenged with seeing if you can get that complex Machine Learning or Deep Learning system to work correctly, your focus becomes solving that problem. It's what is exciting to do and usually via your training and education it is the technology that is the primary focus for you.

When I used to be a university professor teaching computer science and AI classes, I found that trying to include aspects of the ethical or moral considerations often generated backlash, in spite of the rather bland manner of simply raising awareness that the tech being built could have ethical and moral consequences. The mainstay of the backlash was that for every minute of class time spent on discussing the ethical or moral aspects was a minute less devoted to honing the technical skills and capabilities of the students. The key, I was told, was to ensure the students had the highest and purist form of technical skills, and the assumption was that any ethical or moral elements involved would be either self-evident to them or it was something that would come up later on, once they became practitioners of their craft.

Today, we've recently seen the backlash against some of the major social media firms and the online search firms for how their technology seems to imbue ethical or moral aspects. At times, these firms have offered that they are merely technologists and the technology speaks for itself, so to speak. If one assumes that the AI developers weren't purposely embedding ethical and moral sentiments, it nonetheless does not provide an escape from the aspect that those embeddings may exist. In other words, whether purposely placed or not, if they are there it is something that the rest of the world will assert that something needs to be done about it.

And so there is a move afoot to try and inspire AI developers and firms making and promulgating AI systems to become more cognizant of the ethical and moral elements in such systems. For those that didn't think about it before and merely let things happen by perchance or happenstance, this kind of out-of-mind rationalization is gradually disappearing as an excuse for producing an AI system that does have ethical or moral elements and yet for which no overt effort was made to contend with them.

Let's combine together the aspects of AI systems that have ethical or moral elements and/or consequences with the notion that there are international differences in ethics and moral choices and preferences.

If you are an AI developer in country X, and you are developing an AI system, you might fall into the mental trap of crafting that AI system as based on your own cultural norms of being in country X. This means that you might by default be embedding into the AI system the ethics or moral elements that are let's say acceptable in that country X.

This at first might not be even noticed by you. You are doing this without any particular conscious thought or attempt to bias the AI system. It is merely a natural consequence of your ingrained cultural norms as a member of country X. It would be the same as making a system that has as a list of proper foods to eat things like say chicken and burgers. It doesn't even occur to you to add to the list things like ants or termites. In this case, you've silently and unknowingly carried your cultural norm into the AI system.

I've developed quite a number of global systems that had to work throughout the world, and in so doing, I've often been faced with taking an existing system that was successful in say the United States and trying to make it usable in other countries too. It can be challenging to retrofit something to accommodate other cultures and peoples. The number of concrete-like features and assumptions in an AI system can be so deeply embedded that you almost need to start over, rather than simply trying to make adjustments here and there.

I've written and spoken extensively about the internationalizing of AI, of which the ethics and morals dimension are often regrettably neglected by AI developers and AI firms. It is relatively easy to modify an AI system so that it makes use of another language, such as switching it from using English to using Spanish or German as a language. You can also relatively easily change the use of dollar amounts and make them into other forms of currencies. These are the somewhat obvious go-to aspects when trying to internalize software.

The tricky part is ferreting out the ethics and morals elements that are perhaps deeply embedded into the AI system.

You need to figure out what those elements are, which might not have ever come up previously regarding the system and therefore the initial hunch is that there aren't any such embeddings. Usually, once the realization becomes more apparent that there are such embeddings, it then becomes an arduous chore of identifying where those embeddings are, along with what kind of effort and cost will be required to change them.

Even more so as a difficulty is often deciding what to change those embeddings to, regarding what is the appropriate target set of ethics and morals embeddings.

Part of the reason that figuring out the desired target of ethics and moral embeddings is that you often didn't do so at the start anyway. In other words, you never initially had to endure the difficulty of trying to figure out what ethics and moral embeddings you were going to put into the AI system. As such, now that you found them, trying to identify how to change them will finally bring to the surface the hard choices that need to be made.

There is another factor too that comes to play, namely whether the AI system is a real-time one, and whether it has any serious or severe consequences in what it does. The more that the AI system operates in real-time and has potential life-or-death choices to make, if this also dovetails into the ethics or moral embeddings realm, it is a twofer. The ethics or moral embeddings are of a greater significance, whether the AI developer realizes it or not, because life-or-death results can occur and do so as a result of those hidden ethics or morals embeddings.

What does this have to do with AI self-driving cars?

At the Cybernetic AI Self-Driving Car Institute, we are developing AI software for self-driving cars. Auto makers and tech firms are faced with the dilemma of how to have the AI make life-or-death driving choices, and these choices could be construed as being based on ethics or morals elements, of which those can differ by country and culture.

Allow me to elaborate.

I'd like to first clarify and introduce the notion that there are varying levels of AI self-driving cars. The topmost level is considered Level 5.

A Level 5 self-driving car is one that is being driven by the AI and there is no human driver involved. For the design of Level 5 self-driving cars, the auto makers are even removing the gas pedal, brake pedal, and steering wheel, since those are contraptions used by human drivers. The Level 5 self-driving car is not being driven by a human and nor is there an expectation that a human driver will be present in the self-driving car. It's all on the shoulders of the AI to drive the car.

For self-driving cars less than a Level 5, there must be a human driver present in the car. The human driver is currently considered the responsible party for the acts of the car. The AI and the human driver are co-sharing the driving task. In spite of this co-sharing, the human is supposed to remain fully immersed into the driving task and be ready at all times to perform the driving task. I've repeatedly warned about the dangers of this co-sharing arrangement and predicted it will produce many untoward results.

Let's focus herein on the true Level 5 self-driving car. Much of the comments apply to the less than Level 5 self-driving cars too, but the fully autonomous AI self-driving car will receive the most attention in this discussion.

Here's the usual steps involved in the AI driving task:

- Sensor data collection and interpretation
- Sensor fusion
- Virtual world model updating
- AI action planning
- Car controls command issuance

Another key aspect of AI self-driving cars is that they will be driving on our roadways in the midst of human driven cars too. There are some pundits of AI self-driving cars that continually refer to a utopian world in which there are only AI self-driving cars on the public roads. Currently there are about 250+ million conventional cars in the United States alone, and those cars are not going to magically disappear or become true Level 5 AI self-driving cars overnight.

Indeed, the use of human driven cars will last for many years, likely many decades, and the advent of AI self-driving cars will occur while there are still human driven cars on the roads. This is a crucial point since this means that the AI of self-driving cars needs to be able to contend with not just other AI self-driving cars, but also contend with human driven cars. It is easy to envision a simplistic and rather unrealistic world in which all AI self-driving cars are politely interacting with each other and being civil about roadway interactions. That's not what is going to be happening for the foreseeable future. AI self-driving cars and human driven cars will need to be able to cope with each other. Period.

Returning to the topic of ethics and moral elements embedded in AI systems, let's take a closer look at how this plays out in the case of AI self-driving cars and especially in a global context.

Those within the self-driving car industry are generally aware of something that ethicists have been bantering around called the Trolley problem.

Philosophers and ethicists have been using the Trolley problem as a mental experiment to try and explore the role of ethics in our daily lives. In its simplest version, the Trolley problem is that you are standing next to a train track and the train is barreling along and heading to a juncture where it can take one of two paths. In one path, it will ultimately strike and kill five people that are stranded on the train tracks. On the other path there is one person. You have access to a track switch that will divert the train from the five people and instead steer it into the one person. Would you do so? Should you do so?

Some say that of course you should steer the train toward the one person and away from the five people.

The answer is "obvious" because you are saving four lives, which is the net difference of killing the one person and yet saving the five people. Indeed, some believe that the problem has such an apparent answer that there is nothing ethically ambiguous about it at all.

Ethicists have tried numerous variations to help gauge what the range and nature of our ethical decision-making is. For example, suppose I told you that the one person was Einstein and the five people were all evil serial killers. Would it still be the case that the saving of the five and the killing of the one is so easily ascertained by the sheer number of lives involved?

Another variable manipulated in this mental ethical experiment involves whether the train is by-default going toward the five people or whether it is by-default going toward the one person.

Why does this make a difference? In the case of the train by default heading toward the five people, you must take an overt action to avoid this calamity and pull the switch to divert the train toward the one person. If you take no action, the train is going to kill the five people.

Suppose instead that the train was by default heading toward the one person. If you decide to take no action, you have already in essence saved the five people, and only if you actually took any action would the five be killed. Notice how this shifts the nature of the ethical dilemma. Your action or inaction will differ depending upon the scenario.

We are on the verge of asking the same ethical questions of AI self-driving cars. I say on the verge, but the reality is that we are already immersed in this ethical milieu and just don't realize that we are. What actions do we as a society believe that a self-driving car should take to avoid crashes or other such driving calamities? Does the Artificial Intelligence that is driving the self-driving car have any responsibility for its actions?

One might argue that the AI is no different than what we expect of a human driver. The AI needs to be able to make ethical decisions, whether explicitly or not, and ultimately have some if not all responsibility for the driving of the car.

Let's take a look at an example.

Suppose a self-driving car is heading down a neighborhood street. There are five people in the car. A child suddenly darts out from the sidewalk and into the street. Assume that the self-driving car is able to detect that the child has indeed come into the street.

The AI self-driving car is now confronted with an ethical dilemma akin to the Trolley problem. The AI of the self-driving car can choose to hit the child, likely killing the child, and save the five people in the car since they will be rocked by the accident but not harmed, or the self-driving car's AI can swerve to avoid the child but doing so puts the self-driving car onto a path into a concrete wall and will likely lead to the harm or even death of many or perhaps all of the five people in the car. What should the AI do?

Similar to the Trolley problem, we can make variants of this child-hitting problem. We can make it that the default is that the five will be killed and so the AI must take an action to avoid the five and kill the one. Or, we can make the default that the AI will without taking any action kill the one and must take action to avoid the one and thus kill the five. We are assuming that the AI is "knowingly" involved in this dilemma, meaning that it realizes the potential consequences.

When people are asked what they would do, the answer you get will greatly depend upon how you've asked the question.

One of the most significant factors that seems to alter a person's answer is whether you depict the problem in an abstract way without offering any names per se versus if you tell the person that they or someone they know is involved in the scenario.

In the case of the problem being abstract, the person seems likely to answer in a manner that offers the least number of deaths that might arise. If you tell the person that they are let's say inside the self-driving car, they tend to shift their answer to aim at having the car occupants survive. If you tell the person they are outside the self-driving car and standing on the street, and will be run over, they tend to express that the AI self-driving car should swerve, even if it means the likely death of some or all of the self-driving car occupants.

I mention this important point because there are a lot of these kinds of polls and surveys that seem to be arising lately, partially because AI self-driving cars continue to increase in attention to society, and the manner of how the question is asked can dramatically alter the poll or survey results. This explains too why one poll or survey appears to at times have quite different results than another.

You also need to consider who is answering these poll or survey questions.

There is a famous example of how you can inadvertently enlist bias into a survey or poll by whom you select to take it.

In 1936, one of the largest ever at-the-time polls was conducted by a highly respected magazine called The Literary Digest, involving calling nearly 2 ½ million people in the USA to ask them whether they were going to vote for Alfred Landon or Franklin D. Roosevelt for president. The poll results leaned toward Landon and thus The Literary Digest predicted loudly that Landon would win (he did not).

There were at least two problems with the survey approach.

One is that they used a telephone as the medium to reach people, but at the time those that could afford to own a phone were generally the upper-income of society and therefore the survey only got their opinions, having omitted much of the bulk of the voters. Secondly, they started with a list of 10 million names and were only able to reach about one-firth, which implies a non-response bias. In other words, they only talked with those that happened to answer the phone and failed to converse with those that did not happen to answer the phone. It could be that those that answered the phone were a select segment of the larger group for which the survey had hoped to reach and thusly biased the results accordingly.

I hope that you will keep these facets in mind whenever hearing about or reading about a survey of what people say they would do when driving a car. How were the people contacted? What was the depiction of the scenarios? What was the wording of the questions?

Was there a nonresponse bias? Was there a selection bias? And so on.

Another facet involves whether or not the people responding to the questions take the poll or survey seriously. If someone perceives the questions to be silly or inconsequential, they might answer off-the-cuff or maybe even answer in a manner intended to purposely shock the responses or distort the results. You have to consider the motivation and sincerity of those responding.

In the case of AI self-driving cars, there has been an ongoing large-scale effort to try and get a handle on the ethics and moral aspects of making choices when driving a car, via an online experiment referred to as the Moral Machine experiment.

A recent recap of the results accumulated by the online experiment were described in an issue of Nature magazine and indicated that around 2.3 million people had taken the survey. The survey presented various scenarios akin to the Trolley problem and asked the survey respondent what action they would take. There were over 40 million "decisions" that these two million or so respondents rendered in undertaking the survey. Plus, it was undertaken by respondents from 233 countries and territories.

Before I go over the results, I'd like to remind you of the various limitations and concerns about any such kind of survey. Those that went to the trouble to do the online survey were a self-selected segment of society. They had to have online access, which not everyone in the world yet has. They had to be aware that the online survey existed, of which not many people that are online would have known about. They had to be willing to take the time needed to complete the survey. Etc.

We also need to guess that they hopefully took the survey seriously, but we cannot know for sure.

How many of the respondents thought it was a kind of game and didn't care much about how they answered?

How many answered by just clicking buttons and did not give due and somber thought to their answers? How many would change their answers if we altered the depictions of the scenarios and got them to assume that they themselves or a dear loved one was involved in the scenarios?

It's up to you whether you want to toss out the baby with the bathwater in the sense of opting to disregard entirely the results of this interesting online experiment. Admittedly it is hard to just place it aside, given the large number of respondents. Of course, merely that it garnered a lot of responses does not ergo make it valid. You can always get Garbage-In Garbage-Out (GIGO), no matter whether you have a small number or a vast number of responses.

Similar to the Trolley problem, the respondents were confronted with an unavoidable car accident that was going to occur. They were to indicate how an autonomous AI self-driving car should react. I point out this facet since many studies have tended to focus on what the person would do, or what the person thinks other people ought to do, and not per se on what the AI should do.

A fundamental question to be pondered is whether people want the AI to do something other than what they would want people to do.

Often times, these studies assume that if you say that the AI should swerve or not swerve, you are presumably also implying that if it was a person in lieu of the AI that was driving the car, the person is supposed to take that same action. But, perhaps people perceive that the AI should do something for which they don't believe people would do, or maybe even could do.

I'll give you an extreme example, which might seem contrived, but please accept the example to serve as a showcase of how there might be a different kind of viewpoint about the AI as a driver versus a person as a driver.

I tell someone that the scenario involves a parent driving a car, meanwhile the only daughter of the parent has wandered into the street, and the parent regrettably has only a split-second to decide whether to swerve and ram into a wall that will end-up killing the parent, yet doing so will spare the daughter (otherwise, the car will ram and kill the daughter).

That's a tough one, I'd dare say, at least for most people. Can you tell a parent to proceed with killing their own child? I added too that it was the only daughter, which presumably might further increase the agony of the situation.

Let's now augment the scenario and say that the car contains another person. We now have two people in the car, and one person out on the street. If the parent was the only person in the car, I suppose it might be "easier" to say that the parent would or should sacrifice themselves for the life of their child. Now with the change in the scenario, the parent is going to have to make a decision that will also kill the passenger in the car.

Here's where the AI as a driver might enter into the picture. Would your answer about whether the parent should swerve the car differ if the AI was driving the car in this augmented version of the scenario?

If the AI was driving the car and there were no human occupants, I'd suppose we would all likely agree that the AI ought to swerve the car, even if it means smashing into a wall and destroying the car and the AI. Until or if we ever have sentient AI, I don't think we are willing to equate the AI as somehow an equivalent to a human life.

If there is one human passenger in the self-driving car, this implies that the AI will need to make a decision about whether to spare the life of the passenger or to spare the life of the child. Is your answer different if the driver was the parent? I suppose you could say that the case of the parent with a passenger involves two human lives inside the car, while the non-AI instance of the parent driving the car does involve two human lives inside the car.

Of course, the AI driving in a true Level 5 AI self-driving car means that we won't have a human driver as a count of the number of humans inside the car. This adds another twist too to the scenarios. It means that you can have a car that contains only children. I mention this because the usual scenario about the car swerving involves having one or more adults in the car, which would be required in the less than Level 5 scenarios.

In any case, let's try to even out the body counts in case that's your primary focus on making a decision. We'll put the parent in the self-driving car as a passenger, and the AI is driving the car. Should the AI swerve to save the child on the street and in which case it kills the parent?

Would your answer change if I removed the aspect that it was a child of the parent that was standing on the street and said it was some child that the parent did not know? Suppose I said the person standing on the street was an adult and not a child? Suppose I told you that the parent was standing in the street and the child of that parent was in the AI self-driving car?

As you can see, there are a dizzying number of variants and each such variant can potentially change the answer that you might give.

For the large-scale online experiment, here's the kinds of scenarios it used:

- Sparing humans versus sparing animals that are presumed to be pets

- Staying on course straight ahead versus swerving away

- Sparing passengers inside the car versus pedestrians on the roadway

- Sparing more human lives versus fewer human lives

- Sparing males versus females

- Sparing young people versus more elderly people

- Sparing legally-crossing pedestrians versus illegally jaywalking pedestrians

- Sparing those that appear to be physically fit versus those appearing to be less fit

- Sparing those with seemingly higher social status versus those with seemingly lower status

They also added aspects such as in some cases the pretend people depicted in the scenarios were labeled as being medial doctors, or perhaps wanted criminals, or stating that a woman was pregnant, and so on.

These factors were combined in a manner to provide 13 accident pending scenarios to each respondent.

There was also an attempt to collect demographic data directly from the respondents, such as their gender, their age, income, education level, religious affiliation, political preference, and so on.

What makes this study rather special, besides the large-scale nature of it, involves the aspect that the online access was available globally.

This potentially provides a glimpse into the international differences that might come to play in the Trolley problem answers. To-date, most studies have tended to be done within a particular country. As such, it has made it harder to try and compare across countries, which means it has been difficult to compare across cultures, which means it likewise has tended to be difficult to compare across ethics and moral norms.

As an aside, I am not saying that a country is always and only one set of ethics and moral norms. Obviously, a country can contain a diversity of ethics and moral norms. Nonetheless, one could suggest that by-and-large a country in the aggregate is likely to exhibit an overall set of ethics and norms.

The researchers used a statistical technique known as the Average Marginal Component Effect (AMCE) to study the attributes and their impacts. You can quibble about the use of this particular statistical technique, though I'd argue that there are more pronounced quibbles about the selection biases and other factors that more worthwhile to quibble about.

Well, you might wonder, what did the results seem to show?

Respondents tended to spare humans over pets.

I know you might think it should be 100% of humans over pets, but that's not the case. This could be interpreted to suggest that the life of an animal is considered by some cultures and ethics/morals as the equal to a human. Or, it could be that some weren't paying attention to the scenario. Or, it could be that the respondent was fooling around. There are a multitude of interpretations.

You might find of interest that Germany had undertaken a study in 2017 that produced the German Ethics Commission on Automated and Connected Driving report, and rule #7 states that a human life in these kinds of AI self-driving car scenarios is supposed to have a higher priority than do animals.

Should that be a universal principle adopted worldwide and be considered the standard for all AI self-driving cars, wherever those AI self-driving cars might be deployed?

For some, this seems like a no-brainer rule and I'm betting they would say that of course such a rule should be adopted. I'd dare say though that you might find that not everyone agrees with that type of rule.

Overall, these kinds of rules are very hard to get people to discuss, let alone to reach agreement about.

For AI developers, they find themselves between a rock and a hard place. On the one hand, no one seems quite willing to come up with such rules, and yet the AI developers are either by default or by intent going to be embedding such "rules" into their AI systems of their self-driving cars. Down the road (pun!), there will likely be public backlash about how these rules got decided and why they are inside of these AI systems.

The auto makers and tech firms would likely say that if they waited to try and produce AI self-driving cars until the world caught up with figuring out these ethics/morals rules, we probably wouldn't have AI self-driving cars until a hundred years from now, if ever, since you would have a devil of a time with getting people to come together and reach agreement on these rather thorny matters.

Meanwhile, the push and urge to move forward with AI self-driving cars is still moving ahead. Some suggest that AI self-driving cars need to be have a disclosure available as to what assumptions were made in the AI in terms of these kinds of ethics/morals rules. Presumably, if you buy a Level 5 AI self-driving car, you ought to get a full disclosure statement that inform you about these embedded rules.

What about when you get into a ridesharing AI self-driving car?

Some would say that you ought to receive a list of the same kinds of disclosures. Since your life and the lives of others are at stake, you ought to be informed as to what the AI self-driving car is going to potentially do. You might choose to use someone else's ridesharing AI self-driving car that has a different set of ethics/morals rules, because it better aligns with your own viewpoints.

Indeed, it is believed that ultimately, we might see AI self-driving cars being marketed based on the kinds of ethics/morals rules that a particular brand or model encompasses. If you want the version that considers animals to be the equal to humans, you can get the auto maker Y's brand or model, otherwise you'd get auto maker Z's brand or model.

I realize that some would claim that with the Over-the-Air (OTA) electronic communication capability, presumably the auto maker or tech firm can via the cloud merely send an update or patch to your AI self-driving car so that it embodies whatever set of ethics/morals rules you prefer. I don't think this is going to be so easy as you think. Besides the technological aspect of doing so, which can be figured out, though for most of today's AI self-driving cars its going to be quite a retrofit to make this viable, you have other societal questions to deal with.

Maybe you live in a community that believes humans and animals should be considered equal. Maybe you don't see things this way.

Meanwhile, you purchase an AI self-driving car that has an embedded rule that humans are a higher priority than animals. This aligns with your personal sense of ethics and morals. You want to have your AI self-driving car parked at your home in your community and have it drive you throughout your community. You also want to make some money with your AI self-driving car and so you have it work as a ridesharing AI self-driving car when you are not using it.

The community bans the use of that particular model/brand of AI self-driving car. They won't let it be used on their roads. Yikes, you are caught in quite a bind. Even if the auto maker or tech firm has an easy plug-in that can be sent via OTA to implant AI rules about humans and animals being considered equals, you don't share that belief.

I hope I've made the case that we are heading towards a showdown about the ethics/morals embedded rules in AI self-driving cars. It isn't happening now because we don't have true Level 5 AI self-driving cars. Once we do have them, it will be a while before they become prevalent. My guess is that no one is going to be willing to put up much effort and energy to consider these matters until it becomes day-to-day reality and people realize what is occurring on their streets, under their noses, and within their eyesight.

Note that I got us into this whole back-and-forth discussion by merely the topic of the online experiment responses regarding humans versus animals.

Imagine how many other such globally variant perspectives and issues that are that have yet to be identified and debated!

Let's take a look at some more results of the Moral Machine online experiment.

Respondents tended to spare humans by saving more rather than less.

This is the classic viewpoint of all human lives being equal and so it becomes whether or not the number of lives lost can be made less than the number of lives saved. As mentioned earlier, this can be potentially altered in terms of responses based on whether the person believes themselves to be in the "lost" versus the "saved" segment of the scenario. It can also differ if a loved one or someone that you know is considered in one of the segments or the other.

Another factor can be the age of the people in the pretend scenarios.

Generally, the respondents tended to spare a baby, or a little girl, or a little boy, more so than adults.

For some of you, depending upon your culture and ethics/morals, you might contend that it is best to spare a child over an adult, perhaps since you might say that the adult has already lived their life and the child has yet to do so. Or it could that you simply believe that longevity is the key, and an adult has statistically less years left to live over a child.

I'd bet that there are others of you that depending upon your culture and ethics/morals would assert that the adult should usually be the one spared. The adult can readily produce another child. Children historically in the world have been considered at risk in terms of having larger birth rates to deal with the perishing of children due to natural survival aspects. Some say this is why there has been declining birth rates for industrialized nations for which the child survival rates tend to be higher.

I am not trying to resolve the question about age as a factor. I am instead attempting to emphasize that it is yet another unsolved problem. It is unsolved meaning that an AI developer has no means to seemingly know what or how they should direct the AI system to act or react in such circumstances.

An AI self-driving car is driving down the street. Via the cameras and visual image processing, it detects a baby has crawled into the street. At this juncture, should the AI consider this to be a human, and set aside the age aspect, meaning ignore that it is a baby. Of course, when I say ignore, don't go whole hog, in the sense that the AI ought to be programmed to realize that a baby crawls and doesn't run, and therefore be able to predict the movements of the baby.

I am saying "ignore" in the sense that if the AI needs to balance the lives of a choice about swerving the self-driving car, and if there are say two passengers in the self-driving car, it now has a simple math of one human in the street versus two humans inside the self-driving car. Suppose too that the AI has already scanned the interior and has detected that the two passengers are adults.

Once again, we need to ask, should the AI not take notice of the age as a factor and instead merely count them as two people.

We have returned again to the "rules" that would be embedded into the AI system. Those of you that say there aren't any rules in your AI system, this is a bit of a false or at best misleading claim. The omission of a rule means that the AI is going to end-up doing something and the unspecified "rule" is there whether it is explicitly stated or not.

Suppose you are an AI developer and your AI system for your brand of self-driving cars merely counts people as people. There is no distinction about age. Guess what, you have a rule! You have left out age as a factor. Thus, you have a rule that people are counted only as people and that age is not considered.

You might complain that you never even contemplated using age. It did not occur to you to ponder whether age should be a factor in your AI system and its action planning determinations. Does this get you off the hook? Sorry, that won't cut the mustard. There are those that will say that you should have considered including age. You apparently by default either consciously or not have made a decision that the AI will not include age in choosing among people when caught in an untoward situation.

Furthermore, imagine that some country decides they want to allow only AI self-driving cars in their country that do take into account the age of a person when making these horrific kinds of untoward decisions. I know some will say they could adjust their AI code with one line and it would then encompass the age factor. I doubt this. The odds are that there is a lot more throughout the AI system that would need to be altered, along with doing careful testing before you deploy such a life-or-death crucial new change.

There are a number of other results of the online experiment that are indicative of the difficult AI ethics/morals discussions we yet are to confront.

For example, there was a preference of sparing those more physically fit over those that were less physically fit.

How does that strike you? Some might be enraged. How terrible! Others might try to argue that in a Darwinian way that those more physically fit are best to survive. This is the kind of dividing line that definitely rankles us all and brings to the forefront our ethics/morals mores and preferences.

In statistically analyzing the individuals and their demographics, the researchers claim that there are only marginal differences in the rendered opinions of the respondents. For example, you might assume that perhaps male respondents might tend to prefer to save males more so than females, or maybe save females more so than males, but according to the researchers the individual variations were not striking. They suggest that the individual differences are theoretically interesting and yet not essential for policy making matters.

In terms of countries, the researchers opted to try and undertake a cluster analysis that incorporated Ward's minimum variance method and used Euclidean distance calculations related to the AMCE's of each country, doing so to see if there were any significant differences in the country-based results.

They came up with three major clusters, which they named as Western, Eastern, and Southern. The Western cluster was mainly encompassing countries that has Protestant, Catholic and Orthodoxy underpinnings, such as the United States and Europe. The Eastern cluster consisted of the Islamic and Confucian oriented cultures, including Japan, Taiwan, Saudi Arabia, and others. The Southern cluster was indicated as having a stronger preference result for sparking females in comparison to the Western and Eastern clusters, and encompassed South America, Central America, and others.

For AI self-driving cars, the researchers suggest that this kind of clustering might mean that the AI will need to be adjusted accordingly to those dominant ethics/morals in each respective cluster. If one is to assume that the three clusters are a valid means to consider this problem, it could be handy in that it might imply that there are only three major sets of AI "rules" that would need to be formulated to accommodate much of the globe. This seems like quite wishful thinking and I frankly doubt you can lump things together to make this problem into such an easy solution.

When I speak at conferences and bring up this topic of the AI ethics/morals underlying split second life-or-death decisions that an AI self-driving car might need to make, I often get various glib replies. Let me share those with you.

One reply is that we can just let people decide for themselves what kind of ethics/moral judgement the AI should make. Rather than trying to come up with overall policies and infusing those into the AI, just let each person decide what they prefer.

I inquire gently about how this would work. I get into a ridesharing AI self-driving car. It is a blank slate about the ethics/rules of what to do when it gets into an untoward situation. Somehow, the AI starts to ask me about my preferences. Do I care about humans versus animals, it asks. Do I care about adults versus children, it asks. Apparently, I am to be walked through a litany of such questions and once I've answered the questions, the AI will start to take me on my driving journey.

The person that has brought up this topic will usually say that I've been unfair in making it seem like a long wait before the ridesharing car would get underway. It could be that my smartphone would already have my driving preferences and it would convey those to the ridesharing AI self-driving car. Within the time it takes for me to sit down and put on my seat belt, the AI would already know what my preferences are and have them setup for the driving journey.

This sounds nifty. We are back though to the earlier example of a community that has decided they want to consider humans and animals to be equal in merit. Can I just drive in this AI self-driving car into their community and do so while knowing that my preferences violate their preferences?

My point is that these kinds of preferences are not about things like whether the self-driving car should honk its horn or not. These are life-and-death choices about what the self-driving car will do. It involves not just the person that happens to be in the self-driving car, but also has consequences for anyone else in nearby cars and for pedestrians and others.

Another comment I get is that these are dire driving scenarios that will never arise and the whole ethics/morals question is a bogus topic.

When I gently ask about this claim, the person making the remark will usually say that in the thirty years of their driving a car, they have never encountered such a scenario as having to choose between swerving to hit a child versus ramming into a wall with the car. Never. To them, these are wild conjectures.

You might as well be discussing what to do when a meteor from outer space lands smack dab in front an AI self-driving car. What will the AI do about that?

I could point out that dealing with a sudden appearance of a meteor is actually something the AI system ought to already generally be able to handle. I'm not saying that there are AI developers right now programming self-driving cars to be on the watch for flaming meteors. If you consider that a meteor is simply an object that has suddenly appeared in front of the AI self-driving car, which could be equated to a tree limb that has been blown down by the wind or it could equated be a rooftop satellite dish that came tumbling down because of an earthquake, these are all aspects that the AI should be able to deal with.

It is debris that has appeared in front of the AI self-driving car. Until or if we had the human lives choices into the equation, this is just a maneuverability aspect of the AI trying to safety navigate around or otherwise deal with this object or obstacle.

Anyway, I digress. Let's get back to the notion that these scenarios of having to choose between one terribly bad outcome versus another terribly bad outcome is allegedly not realistic and won't happen.

I try to emphasize to the person that just because in their thirty years of driving that they have not encountered such a situation is not appropriate cause to extrapolate that it never happens anywhere and to anyone else. Let's suppose the person drives around 1,000 miles per month, which is the overall average in the United States. This means that over 30 years the person has driven perhaps 30 x 1000 x 12 miles, which calculates to about 360,000 miles in their lifetime so far.

We'd likely want to find out where this person has been driving. If they are driving in the same places most of the time, that's another factor as to whether or not they might be experiencing these kinds of scenarios. In some areas it could happen frequently, in other areas only in a blue moon.

The thing is that there are about 3.22 trillion miles driven in the United States each year (according to the Federal Highway Administration). Over thirty years we might suggest it is about 100 trillion miles of driving. This particular person that made the remark has driven a teensy-weensy fraction of those miles. Their assumption that since they did not experience any such dire situation is a rather bold claim when compared to all of the driving that takes place.

A reasonable person would concede that these scenarios can happen, and they are not impossible. The next aspect is to then discuss whether they are probable or only possible. In other words, yes, they can happen, but they are perhaps very rare.

If you are willing to say that they happen, but are rare, you've now gotten yourself into a pickle. I mention this because if it can happen and if the AI encounters such a situation, what do you want the AI to do? Based on the belief that it rarely happens, are you saying that it is okay if the AI randomly makes a choice or otherwise does nothing systematic to make the choice? I don't think we would want automation for which we know it will ultimately encounter dire situations, but we decided to not stipulate what is to occur.

I also would like to clarify that these extreme examples such as the Trolley problem are meant to spark awareness about the aspect that these overall such situations can arise. Don't become preoccupied with the child in the street and the passengers in the self-driving car as an example. We can come up with many other such examples. Take a situation involving humans inside a car, and have that car come across a pedestrian, or several pedestrians, or a bicyclist, or a bunch of bicyclists, or another car with people in it, and so on.

When you take a moment to consider your daily driving, you are likely to realize that you are quite a bit making life-or-death decisions about driving and that those decisions encompass a kind of moral compass. The moral compass is based on your own personal ethics/morals, along with whatever the stated or implied ethics/morals are in the place that you are driving, and this all gets baked together into your mind as you are driving a car.

I'm not always successful in making the case to such doubters that we need to care about the ethics/morals rules and their embedding into AI systems. A tempest in a teapot is what some seem to believe, no matter what other arguments are presented. There are some too that believe it is a conspiracy of some kind, intended to either holdback the advent of AI self-driving cars or maybe trick us into letting AI self-driving cars on-their-own determine our ethics/morals for us.

Conclusion

The advent of AI self-driving cars raises substantive aspects about how the AI will be making split-second decisions of a real-time nature involving multi-ton cars that can cause life-or-death consequences to humans within the self-driving car and for other humans nearby in either other cars or as pedestrians or in other states of movement such as via bicycles, scooters, motorcycles, etc.

We humans make these kinds of judgements while we are driving a car. Society has gotten used to this stream of judgements that we all make. The expectation is that the human driver will use their judgement as shaped around the culture of the place they are driving and as based on the prevalent ethics/morals therein. When someone gets into a car incident and makes such choices, we are often sympathetic to their plight since the person typically had only a split-second to decide what to do.

We aren't likely to consider that the AI has an excuse that the decision made was time-boxed into a split second. In other words, the AI ought to have beforehand been established to have some set of ethics/morals rules that guide the overarching decision making and then in a moment when a situation arises, we would expect the AI to apply those rules.

You can bet that any AI self-driving car that gets into an untoward situation and makes a choice or by default takes an action that we would consider a form of choice, this is going to be second-guessed by others. Lawyers will line-up to go after the auto makers and tech firms and get them to explain how and why the AI did whatever it opted to do.

The auto makers and tech firms would be wise to systematically pursue the embodiment of ethics/morals rules into their AI systems rather than letting it happen by chance alone. The head-in-the-sand defense is likely to lose support by the courts and the public. From a business and cost perspective, it will be a pay me know or pay me later kind of aspect for the auto makers, namely either invest now to get this done properly or later on pay a likely much higher price that they didn't do it right at the start.

Another way to consider this matter is to take into account the global market for AI self-driving cars. If you are developing your AI self-driving car just for the U.S. market right now, you'll later on kick yourself that you didn't put in place some core aspects that would have made going global a lot easier, less costly, and more expedient. In that sense, the embodiment of the ethics/rules needs to be formulated in a manner that would allow for accommodating different countries and different cultural norms.

The Moral Machine online experiment needs to be taken with a grain of salt. As mentioned, as an experiment it is suffers from the usual kinds of maladies that any survey or poll might encounter. Nonetheless, I applaud the effort as a wake-up call to bring attention to a matter that otherwise is going to be sadly untouched until it is at a point of becoming an utter morass and catastrophe for the emergence of AI self-driving cars. AI self-driving cars are going to be a kind of "moral machine" whether you want to admit it or not. Let's work on the morality of the moral machine sooner rather than later.

CHAPTER 6

COMPUTATIONAL PERISCOPY

AND

AI SELF-DRIVING CAR

CHAPTER 6

COMPUTATIONAL PERISCOPY

AND

AI SELF-DRIVING CAR

The Shadow knows!

That was the famous line used in the popular pulp novel series, comic book series, and radio series about a fictional character known as The Shadow. If you are familiar with the mysterious legacy of this clad-in-black superhero-like vigilante, you likely know that preceding the exclamation was a question essentially asking what evil lurks nearby. Eventually, the popular expression "the shadow knows" has become an integral part of our global lexicon and often used as an idiom to express being able to magically or inexplicably know what is going on.

We tend to not particularly notice our own shadow. How often do you glance around to see your own shadow? Probably not very frequently. I'd bet you tend to ignore other people's shadows too. Unless you happen to a landscapes painter or a photographer, the odds are that you take shadows for granted. I'm not faulting you for any lack of attention to shadows, since they usually don't seem to do much or have any special purpose.

There are times though when a shadow can be a very handy thing.

I remember when my children were quite young that we devised a clever and fun hide-and-seek kind of game at the local playground, and, as I'll mention in a moment, shadows became a crucial aspect to be paid attention to.

This playground had very few sizable objects and thereof was absent of anything notable for us to hide behind. You could not hide behind the swings, nor could you hide behind the climbing posts. You would have to be paper thin to use those as objects to hide behind. Fortunately, with a great insight by the kids, we jointly came up with a hide-and-seek game based on a handball wall that was there at the playground.

The handball wall allowed people to play handball on either side of the wall (it was a free-standing wall). People would stand on one side, and with their hands slightly cupped, they would bat a small ball against the wall. One person would bat at the ball and then the other player would bat at the ball. This is an obviously simplified description of the sport of handball and I am assuming that you know what handball consists of.

In any case, the wall could serve as a means to hide. At first glance, it seemed like a rather silly object to hide behind. There was just the one wall, standing by itself in an open and plain asphalt area or pad, and nothing else was nearby. If you hid "behind" the wall, it would mean that you would be standing merely on the other side of the wall that the person seeking you was not standing at. The seeker could immediately find you by just walking around the either end of the wall and voila you've been caught. Not much of a hide-and-seek.

We put our heads together to devise a more viable means to use the wall as a hiding obstacle, since it was the only viable place to "hide" and therefore play hide-and-seek.

Here's what we came up with.

We considered this version of hide-and-seek to be a two-player game. One of my children would stand on one side of the wall and position themselves at the mid-point of the wall. I would stand on the other side of the wall and also be positioned at the mid-point. At this juncture, we cannot see each other. We are "hidden" from each other by the wall. Yes, I realize it is apparent that we each know where the other one is, but I'll explain how quickly that will change.

Upon yelling out the word "Start!" to get the game underway, the seeker can choose to dart toward either end of the wall, likewise the hider is supposed to dart to either end of the wall, each of us staying for the moment on our respective side of the wall.

Once they each get to the corner of the wall, the seeker needs to decide whether to then go onto the other side of the wall, or instead wait where they are. The seeker is hoping to turn the corner and when doing so will catch the other person (the hider) at that same end of the wall, in which case the seeker wins the game.

If the hider has chosen to rush to the other end of the wall, the seeker upon revealing themselves by coming onto the side where the hider is, will "lose" that round and the game continues. In which case the hider moves to the other side of the wall, namely the side that the seeker just came from. The seeker now can rush to the corner that the hider was just at, or instead stay at the corner they just turned. The seeker will need to try and guess again as to where on the other side the hider is now positioned.

Maybe this sounds complicated, but I assure you it is a quite simple and easy version of hide-and-seek.

There are fun strategies you can employ and for which I believe boosted their cognitive skills, in addition to the physical exercise of running back-and-forth.

One trick involved the use of deception, in which you might try to make a lot of noise with your feet as though you are running along the wall in a particular direction, doing so to perhaps fool the other person into guessing which corner you are heading toward. You can also run to one corner and turn around and run back to the other corner, doing so repeatedly, on your side of the wall, as a means to confound your opponent.

Admittedly, this game only works well with very young children. An adult having any keen sense of sound and motion can pretty much figure out where the other person is. The great thing about small children is that they are willing and eager to play along and enjoy the game. We would play this hide-and-seek seemingly endlessly.

There is another interesting element and that is the classic tit-for-tat strategy that can be used. The kids would try to outthink me in terms of where I was going to be. If during the last round I had right away gone to the corner at the northern edge, maybe this implied that on the next round I would go to the same edge. Or, maybe I figured they figured that's what I would do, and so they figured that I would purposely not go to that edge, since I was trying to trick them. I relished that this taught them the tit-for-tat aspects.

After playing the game many times, I detected something that I wondered if the children had yet figured out.

When you stood at a corner of the wall, it was possible that your shadow would be cast and therefore the person on the other side of the wall would know where you were standing. Without having to actually try and peek around the corner, you could just quietly tiptoe up to the corner and see if there was a shadow there.

The shadow knows!

Since we each were supposed to end-up at the respective corners, you could pretty much look for a shadow and if you did see one then the person was standing at that corner, while if you were at the corner where there wasn't a shadow cast you could deduce that the person wasn't at that corner (an exception being if the person was rushing from one side to the other at the moment that you tried to look for a shadow).

This also meant that your own shadow could possibly give you away. As such, I would at times drop down to my belly or crouch, trying to minimize the size of my shadow, when standing at any of the corners. I remember even thinking that maybe I could go grab a tree branch and put it at a corner as a means to cast a shadow and trick the seeker into believing I was standing or crouching there. It would have been at best a one-time trick and so I opted not to try it.

The shadow detection ploy was not guaranteed since it all depended upon where the sun was in relation to the position of the wall. Throughout a day, the shadow casting would obviously change as the sun moved across the sky. You might think of the wall as a giant kind of sundial. You could nearly tell the time of day by how the shadow cast off the wall. Per weather conditions, the shadow might not appear at all if the sky was filled with clouds, or the shadow was so minimized that you could not discern it, thus you could not rely upon the shadow as a means of "cheating the system" (well, was it cheating or just darned clever to use the shadows in this manner?).

I debated in my own mind whether I should reveal the shadow trickery to the kids. Once revealed, it was relatively easy to defeat the shadow maneuver and so neither of us could likely rely upon it again. On the other hand, when my children played the game against other children, I wanted to make sure they had every trick up their sleeve and also that they would not be tricked by other children. That's the father in me. My kids first.

Well, it turns out they figured out the shadow trick on their own (probably best way to do so!). Unless either player got sloppy, the shadow no longer mattered. But, there was a chance that the other player in their haste and excitement might neglect to pay attention to the shadows, in which case it was still possible to use it as a game playing advantage.

As the children got older, they eventually in school read the famous "Allegory of the Cave" that Plato had included into his collection of writings known as the Republic. Did you read it while you were in grade school or maybe later on in college?

I bring it up because it is all about shadows.

The fascinating and allegorical story consists of people that are chained inside a cave and can never leave the cave. The manner of how they are chained is such that they must face a wall of the cave. They can only look at the wall. They cannot turn away from the wall. Their gaze is only focused at the wall. You might quibble with this premise and wonder how someone could live their life in this manner, but just go with the flow and try not to butt heads with it.

Behind the people that are chained-up and living in the cave is a controlled fire. The people cannot directly see the fire. They cannot look behind themselves. They can only gaze forward at the wall in front of them.

Anyone or anything that goes behind the chained people will via the light from the fire have a shadow cast upon the wall of the cave. The only experience that these people have about the world is entirely based on the shadows cast onto the cave wall. They opt to give names to the shadows. Their entire belief system about reality is based entirely on the shadows that they see on the cave wall.

You can imagine for a moment the weird things that you might believe about the world if you only experienced the world via these shadows. Keep in mind that we are going with the story as is. Those chained-up people are raised from birth in this manner and they have no other contact with the outside world. Even the people and objects brought into the cave are only seen by these people via the shadows.

Could you know what a tree is, assuming that you never saw an actual tree, and only knew about a tree via the shadow of the tree? Could you know what a dog is, having only seen it via the shadow of the dog?

It's a quite interesting thought experiment, brought to you by Plato. Clever of him.

The practitioners reading this story by Plato might find it preposterous and see little value in the story. There are lots of ways to interpret what he was trying to teach us.

One point that seems pertinent herein is that the human condition is bound by the impressions we receive through our senses. We take for granted our senses, until we lose them, or they falter. If you've ever temporarily lost your hearing due to swimming in a pool or maybe going to a loud rock concert, you at that moment might have realized the importance of your ears and being able to hear. It is said that blind people, those blind from birth, perceive the world in a different manner than those that have had sight and the use of their eyes for throughout their existence.

If you carry forward Plato's allegory a bit more, presumably the way in which we come to know things about the world, some would say the epistemological aspects (a theory about knowing and knowledge), becomes shaped by our senses. Our senses provide the input for which our cognition builds mental models about reality. This implies that the nature of the sensory input will shape your cognition and what it crafts as a model of the world.

I'll be saying more about this in quite practical aspects momentarily. I'm not going to go overboard on the Plato aspects and I bring it up to primarily highlight the potential importance of shadows. Maybe that's a relief for those of you that were concerned that this Plato stuff was veering us away from the real-world.

Indeed, I'd like to now introduce the topic of computational periscopy.

I'd wager that many of you might not be familiar with this field of endeavor. It can be directly associated with the hide-and-seek game that I used to play with my children. Handy that we played the game and I perchance mentioned it to you.

The notion of computational periscopy involves the use of a computer-based approach to effectively devise a kind of periscope. We all know that a periscope is normally a physical device that you can use to look around a corner or over the top of an object, doing so without you hopefully being seen. Perhaps you had one when you were a child. These had quite cheap optics and allowed you to be a pretend army soldier.

In computational periscopy, one key area of interest is how to figure out what you cannot directly see, namely when you have non-line-of-sight (NLOS) of something and possibly use other clues to guess at what might be there. How did I try to figure out when my child, acting as a seeker, might be on the other side of the wall and standing at the corner? I had NLOS at that moment of my offspring. As mentioned, I opted to try and use the shadow as a surrogate of what might be on the other side of the wall.

Computational periscopy can try to use that same shadow trick. I forewarned you, the shadow knows! There are additional facets to computational periscopy including considering refracted light, along with intentionally beaming light at objects, but we'll focus herein only on the topic of shadows.

Suppose you have a robot that is meandering around a room. It is trying to navigate the room and do so without bumping into things. Suppose there is a refrigerator standing in the middle of this room. The robot wants to go around the refrigerator. The robot sensors do not allow it to see magically around the refrigerator and thus the robot will come up to the refrigerator and then turn the corner, yet not know what to expect. What might be on the other side of that refrigerator?

Imagine that there is sufficient lighting in the room that shadows are being cast. The image processing of the camera images streaming into the robot "eyes" could analyze the scene and try to determine if there are any shadows being cast beyond the edge of the refrigerator. If so, the robot could try to figure out what kind of object might be on the other side of the refrigerator.

When you consider this shadow analysis for a moment, consider again my hide-and-seek game.

When I was looking to see the shadow of my children, I would have already generally known that the shadow must be their shadow (because there was no one else on the other side of the wall and no other object nearby that would be casting the shadow).

I also knew the height, weight, and overall size of my children. I knew where the sun was in the sky and how shadows were being cast. Based on the size and shape of the shadow, I could deduce that the shadow was being cast by my children.

Remember that I mentioned the idea of my possibly getting tricky and using a tree branch to cast a shadow? If I had done so, the shadow cast by the tree branch would not likely be the same size and shape as the shadow cast by my body (I am not a tree branch, I assure you). Of course, you can distort a shadow and position even a tree branch in a manner that it might cast a shadow similar to the shadow of a person. You've certainly done the classic shadow puppets with your hands, showing a rabbit or a flying dove. We'll all done this, though some more effectively than others.

Let's pretend that I didn't know my child was standing on the other side of the wall. Suppose I could only see the shadow of them. Could I revere engineering from their shadow and try to guess at what most likely is casting the shadow? Sure, this is possible. I likely could have at least guessed the height and shape of the object that was casting the shadow, along with where the object most likely was positioned.

The robot in the room can try to do the same thing. Besides "seeing" objects directly, it can try to guess at the nature and position of objects not seen, if it can detect shadows of the objects. Suppose that a human is standing on the other side of the refrigerator and doing so out-of-sight of the robot (this is the NLOS). Via the lighting in the room, it turns out that the human is casting a shadow. The shadow is visible to the robot. The shadow of this human extends beyond the refrigerator, at the front of it, and lays cast onto the floor area that the robot is about to navigate.

Based on the shadow, the robot using computational periscopy algorithms and techniques would "reverse engineer" from the characteristics of the shadow and estimate that there is a person standing beyond view on the other side of the refrigerator.

Or, maybe the shadow shape is poor, due to the stance of the object and the lighting aspects of the room, and perhaps the robot cannot discern that it might be a human casting the shadow, but it is pretty sure there is something there casting the shadow. The periscopy algorithm might suggest that it is some kind of object that stands about 6 feet in height and has a width of about a foot or two. That's enough of a guess that it permits the robot to be cautious when going around the refrigerator, allowing it to anticipate that there is something standing there and will need to be quickly navigated around too.

Nifty!

Computational periscopy provides another means to collect sensory data and try to make something useful out of it.

I'll tie that to Plato. We use our senses to make sense of the world around us. There are things we detect and things we don't detect, and yet sometimes the things that we detect are useful and yet not well utilized. I earlier said that most of us don't think much about shadows. Most of today's AI systems that are doing image processing are usually discarding any shadow related data. It is not something they are setup to examine.

Sadly, regrettably, this is tossing out some potentially valuable data that can give further clues to the environment in which the AI system is operating. Sometimes any clue is better than no clue. You can argue that the shadows are perhaps not overly helpful or that they are only going to be helpful some of the time, which I well concede, but at the same time if you are trying to push the envelope and get AI to be as good as it can get, squeezing out every ounce of the sensory data might make a significant difference.

Let's not kid ourselves though and assume that shadows are an easy matter to analyze. If you walk around later today and start looking carefully at shadows, you'll realize there is a tremendous variation in how a shadow is being cast. Trying to reverse engineer the shadow to deduce what casted it, well, this can be tough to do. Plus, you are going to end-up usually with probabilities about what might be there or not there, rather than pure certainties.

The other "killer" (downside) aspect right now is that computational periscopy tends to require humongous amounts of computing processing to undertake. Much of the work to-date has soaked up supercomputer time to try and figure out the shadow related aspects. It can be costly to purchase such premium computing power.

There are also the real-time aspects that are daunting too.

If a robot is moving around a room, and if we want it to do so in any reasonable amount of time, sauntering around like a person might, this means that any of the shadow related processing has to happen in near real-time. You are now upping the ante in that the robot has to have supercomputing capability either natively or via other reliable access, and it needs to pump the images into that processing and get back the results in near real-time to make good use of the analyses performed.

In the case of having a rolling robot on say Mars, if the robot is moving one inch every 24 hours, you perhaps might have a greater chance of doing the analyses of the shadows in time for when it is needed. The everyday robot that we envision walking around in our malls, homes, and the like, they aren't going to have that same luxury of being able to move at a snail's pace.

In short, the computational periscopy is handy, yet it still is in need of faster algorthims and improved techniques so that it can readily be used in near real-time situations, along with finding a means to cut back on the computing power needed so that this kind of processing can be done on more everyday hardware.

A recent study at Boston University provides a glimpse at how computational periscopy might ultimately be ready for prime time and be amenable to more mass appeal. Rather than using a specialized ultrafast optical system, which is usually used in these shadow detecting efforts, they instead used a common digital camera. The digital camera was inexpensive, considered ubiquitous, and only utilized 2D. They had a robot include in its navigation scheme the analysis of shadows cast onto a wall. This was done with more mundane computer hardware. If you are interested in the study, they've posted their research data and details on GitHub.

It's a healthy sign that we are hopefully going to be able to move computational periscopy toward being practical and usable for everyday purposes, though the road ahead is still long.

Speaking of roads, I'd like to mention something that happened to me the other day.

I was driving along on a busy street. A delivery truck had decided to double-park. This is dangerous and generally illegal. Anyway, I'm sure you've seen it happen quite frequently. One can be sympathetic to the delivery agent driving the truck that it is often impossible to find a safe and open spot to park a delivery truck, and doing when they are just quickly dropping off a package would make their day dreadfully long, thus it seems "permissible" to do a double parking to get the delivery job done. To clarify, I am not condoning this. It is still dangerous and can lead to injury or harm.

I could not see the delivery driver. I assumed the driver had stepped out of the truck and was dashing to someone's door to make the delivery of a package. The question was whether or when the delivery driver would get back to the truck. They would need to either likely weave their way in front of their own truck and then get into the open cab to start driving to the next destination, or maybe the agent might come around the back of the truck and snake their way along the side of the truck up to the open cab area.

I was zipping along on the street. There was going to be almost no space left between the right-side of my car and the left side of the delivery truck. A salami could barely fit between the two. And that would be at most one slice.

I realize you could say that I should slow down, come to a halt, and wait for the delivery truck driver to return and move the truck out of the way. Preposterous! Like most drivers, I felt that the truck driver was in the wrong, which he was, and I was going to zip down the street and pass his double-parked truck, come heck or high water. Does my urge to drive past at a fast speed mean that there are now two wrongs in this equation? If so, do two wrongs make for a right? Probably not.

My main concern was when and how the truck driver was going to materialize. If he was smart, he would peek out his head to make sure the traffic was clear and then go alongside his double-parked truck to get into the cab. Usually these delivery agents are being clocked to get their deliveries done in time and so the odds are that the driver was going to do what he usually does, namely just go for it and assume that there isn't traffic or that any traffic will not hit him or her.

Sure enough, just as I came alongside the truck, I saw a shadow and a rapid motion at the front of the truck. I mentally calculated that it was presumably the delivery agent, returning to the truck, though I suppose it could be someone else like a jaywalker or maybe a wandering giraffe. Whatever it was, it was something. Because it was something, I figured that I ought to be swerve away and also add some braking to my car to slow down as I came upon whatever or whomever it was.

Turns out that it was the delivery driver. I veered into the opposing lane to avoid him. Fortunately, there wasn't any traffic coming my way. The delivery driver jumped into his cab and tipped his hat in my direction, presumably saying thanks for making his job easier. I nearly thought I should get a reward from the delivery company for having saved the life of the driver. I'm watching my mail to see if I get a nice letter and beefy check from the company (not holding my breath!).

Did you notice an important and relevant word in my narrative about the delivery truck and the saving of the life of the truck driver? You should have. The magical word was "shadow." I had seen the shadow of the truck driver. This clued me that someone or something was potentially coming along. I had been expecting that someone or something might come along, so I was keeping my eyes peeled.

When you are driving a car, you are somewhat unlikely to usually be noticing the shadows around you and your car. As humans, and as car drivers, we typically take shadows for granted. I would even say that there might be some kind of mental processing taking place about shadows and we might not just realize we are doing so. It is like breathing air. You don't give it direct thought.

You are so used to shadows that your mind likely is processing them but most of the time deciding it either isn't worthwhile to put much mental effort toward, or that it will only do so when it becomes necessary.

Have you ever been driving your car on a sunny day, and all of a sudden, a large cloud formation goes in front of the sun? This casts a large shadow onto your car and the road. I'd bet that your mind noticed that something light-related just happened. You might even turn to someone else in your car and say, hey, did you notice that, it all of a sudden got dark. This suggests that your mind is on the alert for shadows, and giving it low priority most of the time, until or if something happens to get the priority pumped up.

What does this have to do with AI self-driving cars?

At the Cybernetic AI Self-Driving Car Institute, we are developing AI software for self-driving cars. One aspect about the visual processing of images coming from the cameras on the self-driving car is that we can potentially boost the AI driving capabilities by making use of computational periscopy, including detecting and analyzing shadows.

Allow me to elaborate.

I'd like to first clarify and introduce the notion that there are varying levels of AI self-driving cars. The topmost level is considered Level 5. A Level 5 self-driving car is one that is being driven by the AI and there is no human driver involved. For the design of Level 5 self-driving cars, the auto makers are even removing the gas pedal, brake pedal, and steering wheel, since those are contraptions used by human drivers. The Level 5 self-driving car is not being driven by a human and nor is there an expectation that a human driver will be present in the self-driving car. It's all on the shoulders of the AI to drive the car.

For self-driving cars less than a Level 5, there must be a human driver present in the car. The human driver is currently considered the responsible party for the acts of the car. The AI and the human driver are co-sharing the driving task. In spite of this co-sharing, the human is supposed to remain fully immersed into the driving task and be ready at all times to perform the driving task. I've repeatedly warned about the dangers of this co-sharing arrangement and predicted it will produce many untoward results.

Let's focus herein on the true Level 5 self-driving car. Much of the comments apply to the less than Level 5 self-driving cars too, but the fully autonomous AI self-driving car will receive the most attention in this discussion.

Here's the usual steps involved in the AI driving task:

- Sensor data collection and interpretation
- Sensor fusion
- Virtual world model updating
- AI action planning
- Car controls command issuance

Another key aspect of AI self-driving cars is that they will be driving on our roadways in the midst of human driven cars too. There are some pundits of AI self-driving cars that continually refer to a utopian world in which there are only AI self-driving cars on the public roads. Currently there are about 250+ million conventional cars in the

United States alone, and those cars are not going to magically disappear or become true Level 5 AI self-driving cars overnight.

Indeed, the use of human driven cars will last for many years, likely many decades, and the advent of AI self-driving cars will occur while there are still human driven cars on the roads. This is a crucial point since this means that the AI of self-driving cars needs to be able to contend with not just other AI self-driving cars, but also contend with human driven cars. It is easy to envision a simplistic and rather unrealistic world in which all AI self-driving cars are politely interacting with each other and being civil about roadway interactions. That's not what is going to be happening for the foreseeable future. AI self-driving cars and human driven cars will need to be able to cope with each other.

Returning to the topic of computational periscopy, let's consider how this innovative approach can be leveraged by AI and especially in the case of AI self-driving cars.

If the use of computational periscopy could aid the AI in being a better driver, we'd certainly want to give this approach a solid chance of being utilized. Admittedly, the odds that the periscopy via shadow detection and interpretation is going to be a dramatic difference in improving driving is somewhat slim. Thus, most AI developers for AI self-driving cars would likely put the periscopy onto an edge problem list, rather than a mainstay problem list.

An edge problem is one that is regarded as sitting at the edge or far corner of the core problem you are trying to solve. Right now, AI developers are focused on getting an AI self-driving car to fundamentally drive the car, doing so safely, and otherwise are covering a rather hefty checklist of key elements involved in achieving a fully automated AI-driving self-driving car. Dealing with shadows would be interesting and would have some added value, but devoting resources and attention to it is not as vital as covering the fundamentals first.

I often disagree with pundits about what they consider to be edge problems for AI self-driving cars. There are too many so-called edge problems that those pundits try to carve out. By carving out seemingly small piece after another, they usually have not only pared things to the barebones, they've also in my view chopped into the bone itself. In essence, with lots of hand waving, they are skipping over edges that are actually integral to core.

For once, in this case of the periscopy, I would tend to agree that it indeed should be considered an edge problem (they'll be happy to know this!).

Now that I've made the confession, don't overstate the edge aspects of periscopy. I believe it nonetheless does add value. I would be so bold to suggest that the second or third generation of true Level 5 AI self-driving cars will consider the adoption of periscopy as a standard item. By then, hopefully most of the difficulties of trying to put in place periscopy will have been ironed out and it will be viable to use it for an AI self-driving car.

I've already mentioned that there are some tough barriers, such as the amount of computer processing needed to carry out the shadow detection and analysis. We are already loading down an AI self-driving with a ton of computer processing capabilities to do the sensor data collection and analysis for the cameras, for the radar, for the LIDAR, for the ultrasonic, and so on. Plus, the sensor fusion needs to bring together all of these sensory analyses and try to balance them, figuring out how they can be pieced together like a jigsaw puzzle to craft a cohesive indication of what's happening surrounding the self-driving car.

Would it be worthwhile to devote processing power to doing the shadow detection and analysis?

Would it be worthwhile to include the shadow analyses into the sensor fusion that is already trying to connect the dots on the other sensory analyses?

If this addition would mean that time delays might occur between sensor data collection to sensor fusion and ultimately to the AI action planner, we'd need to weigh whether that time delay was worth the benefits of doing the shadow analyses. Might not be.

Also, if we are limited to how much computer processing power we can pack into the AI self-driving car, and if the shadow analyses occurred at the sacrifice of using processing power for other efforts, we wouldn't want that to be a consequence either, unless we knew that the shadow analyses had a substantive enough payoff.

You might argue that we can just add more computer processing on-board the self-driving car but doing so continues to raise the cost of the self-driving car, and raises the complexity of the AI system, and adds weight and potential bulk to the car. These are factors that need to be compared on an ROI (Return on Investment) basis as to whatever the shadow detection can likely provide.

Let's set aside for a moment the concerns about the on-board processing and other related factors. It might be helpful to consider the difficulties involved in the shadow detection and analysis. This might also inspire those of you sparked by this problem to help find ways to improve the periscopy algorthims and techniques. It would be handy to get them optimized for being faster, better, and consume less computer processing power and memory. Well, of course that's just about always a goal for any computer application.

Close your eyes and imagine a shadow, whichever one that comes to mind. Or, if you are in place where you easily create a shadow, please do so.

Where did the shadow cast onto? That's important. If you have the shadow casting onto a flat surface like a floor or a wall, it's likely easier to detect. Once the shadow appears on a surface that is irregular, or if the shadow spreads across a multitude of differing surfaces, trying to detect the shadow can become harder to do.

Another aspect is whether you have two objects that each cast a shadow and the shadows intersect or merge with each other. You have to assume that you cannot see the original objects that are casting the shadow. This means that when you are looking at the merged shadow, you cannot readily figure out which portion of the shadow refers to which of the original objects.

I remember putting my children sometimes up on my shoulders when they were toddlers. I would point at the shadow we cast. It looked like the shadow was showcasing some monstrous creature that was over 7 feet tall. If you did not know or could not have guessed what cast the shadow, and you only had the shadow itself, it would be problematic to reverse engineer it and be able to say with any certainty that it was me and my son or daughter on my shoulders.

That being said, if you have some clues or at least guesses about what might be casting a shadow, you can use that to your advantage when trying to decipher the shadow. In the case of the delivery truck driver, I was waiting expectantly for the driver to come back to the double-parked truck. The shadow that appeared was not something I carefully scrutinized. I was betting that whatever shadow appeared, if any, it was a likely signal that the driver was coming back to the truck.

Had I been more like a computer system with a camera, I could have perhaps analyzed the shadow and tried to match it to whatever an adult sized person's shadow at that time of the day in terms of the lighting would cast as a shadow. This might have been handy. Suppose a dog happened along and it was casting the shadow, rather than the driver. The shadow of the dog would likely be different than that of the say 6-foot-tall adult.

Another facet of a shadow involves motion and movement. When I had my children on my shoulders, I would stand still, and we'd look at the shadow. The shadow was relatively stable and clearly seen. I could play tricks by twisting my body, getting the light to cast off a different angle. But what would really make a difference was moving around. By walking or running with them on my shoulders, and with them shifting back-and-forth, the shadow does a kind of dance.

It is going to be more challenging to decipher a dancing shadow. The stationary shadow already has challenges. Add to the shadow that it is moving, along with the aspect that the object can be twisting and turning, you've got yourself quite a shadow detection task.

I'll make things even more intriguing, or shall I say more complex and arduous. We are going to have cameras mounted into the AI self-driving car that are capturing the images or video of what is outside of the self-driving car. The self-driving car can be standing still, such as at a stop sign or red light. The self-driving car is more likely to be in-motion during a typical driving journey.

You now have a series of streaming images, which are being generated while the self-driving car is in motion, and meanwhile you are trying to detect shadows, of which the objects casting those shadows is likely moving to. I hope this impresses you as to the underlying hardness of solving this problem. We should applaud us humans that we seem to be able to do this kind of detection with relative ease. There's a lot more to it than might meet the eye, so to speak.

I would be remiss in not also emphasizing the role of light in all of this. The light source that is casting the shadows can also be in motion. The light source can be blocked, temporarily, while the AI is in the midst of examining a series of images. The light source can get brighter or dimmer. All of the effects of the lighting will consequently impact the shadows.

I had mentioned earlier that we've all had moments while driving a car on a sunny day and a set of clouds blocks momentarily the sun, altering the shadows being cast. Let's combine that aspect with my desire to ascertain if the delivery truck driver was heading back to his truck. Imagine that the moment the driver got to the truck, a cloud floated along, blocking the creation of his shadow.

Just because there is no shadow does not ergo always mean there is no object there. The shadow detection has to take this aspect into account. Likewise, an object that casts a shadow that seems to be unmoving does not necessarily mean the object itself is rooted in place. The shadow of a street sign is likely to be motionless, which makes sense because it is presumably rooted in place. The truck driver might have gotten to the front of his truck and frozen in place, for an instant, which might allow me to detect his shadow, but the stationary aspect of the shadow cannot be used to assert that the object itself will remain stationary.

Shadows got a lot of intense attention by the entertainment industry for purposes of developing more realistic video games. For those of you that remember the bygone days, you know that there was a period of time whereby animated characters in a video game lacked shadows. It was a somewhat minor omission and you could still enjoy playing the game.

Nonetheless, it was well-known within the video gaming industry that game players were subtly aware that there weren't shadows. This made the characters in the game less lifelike. A lot of research on shadows and computer graphics poured into being able to render shadows. The early versions were "cheap" in that the shadow was there but you could discern easily that it wasn't like a real shadow. Sometimes the shadow would magically disappear when it shouldn't. Sometimes the shadow stayed and yet the character had moved along, which was kind of funny to see if you happened to notice it.

Another area of intense interest on shadows involves analyzing satellite images. When you are trying to gauge the height of a building, the building might be partially blocked from view by trees or camouflage. Meanwhile, the shadow might be a telltale clue that is not also obscured. The same thing with people that are standing or sitting or crouching. You can potentially figure out where the people are by looking at their shadows.

I mention this other work about shadows to highlight that the shadow efforts are not solely for doing computational periscopy. There are a lot of good reasons to be thinking about the use of computers for analyzing shadows.

Pretend that you are in a Level 5 AI self-driving car. It is coming up to an intersection. The light is green. The cross-traffic has a red light. The AI assumes that it has right-of-way and proceeds forward under the assumption that the self-driving car can continue unabated into and across the intersection.

There are tall buildings at each of the corners of this intersection. The AI cannot see what's on the other sides of those buildings. This means that there could be cross-traffic approaching the intersection, but the AI could not yet detect the traffic, only once those cars come into view at their respective red-light crosswalk stopping areas.

This might be a handy case of potentially detecting the shadow of a speeding car that is in the cross-traffic and not going to stop at the red light. It all depends on the lighting and other factors. This is though a possibility. I already gave another possibility of the truck driver, a pedestrian for a moment in time, trying to step out from behind a large obstacle, his double-parked truck.

One approach to trying to do a faster or better job at analyzing shadows by an AI system, assuming that a shadow can be found, involves the use of Machine Learning (ML) and Deep Learning (DL).

Conventional computational periscopy algorithms tend to use arcane calculus equations to try and decipher shadows. Another potential approach involves collecting together tons of images that contain shadows and trying to get a Deep Learning artificial convolutional neural network to pattern on those images. Perhaps shadows of a fire hydrant are readily discerned by pattern matching rather than having to calculate the nature of the shadow and reverse engineering back to the shape of a fire hydrant.

The neural network would need to catch onto the notion that the lighting makes a difference in terms of the shadow cast. It would need to catch onto the aspect that the surface of where the shadow is cast makes a difference. And so on.

These though presumably could become part of the neural network pattern matching and ultimately be able to do a quick job of inspecting a shadow to stipulate what it might be and what it might portend for the AI self-driving car.

Conclusion

We can come up with a slew of ways in which shadow detection and analysis could be meaningful while driving a car.

Some human drivers overtly use shadows to their advantage. Most of the time, shadows are quietly there, and the odds are that a human driver is not especially paying attention to them. There can also be crucial moments, a key moment in time, during which a shadow can provide an added clue about a roadway situation that could spell a life-or-death difference.

Recent efforts to forge ahead with computational periscopy are encouraging and illustrate that we might someday be able to get a shadow detection and analysis capability that can function well in real-time, doing so without hogging the computing power available in a self-driving car and nor requiring the Hoover Dam to empower it.

Still, all in all, we have a bumpy and complicated way yet to go.

This shadow detection "trickery" isn't a silver bullet for AI self-driving cars.

On a cloudy day there might not be any discernable shadows. At night time, you might not have any shadows to detect, depending upon the available street lighting. The shadows themselves might be cast onto surfaces that won't show well the shadow, or the shadow is dancing, and you cannot get a good reading on what the size and shape of the shadow is.

We can easily derive a long list of ways in which shadows won't either work or they will have little probative value.

Does the shadow know? I assert that sometimes the shadow does know. Maybe we can use the shadow to avoid the evils of car accidents that lurk on our roadways and await our every move. Bravo, computational periscopy.

CHAPTER 7

SUPERIOR COGNITION

AND

AI SELF-DRIVING CARS

CHAPTER 7

SUPERIOR COGNITION

AND

AI SELF-DRIVING CARS

Too smart for their own good. Smarter than their britches. Egghead. Pointy head. Einstein. These are the kinds of polite slurs that are sometimes used to takedown someone that seems to be highly intelligent.

This can be especially lobbed whenever the person evokes the know-it-all kind of stance and tries to lord over others with their professed smartness and smarty-pants attitude. Not everyone that might be in the intellectual high-end rankings is necessarily the type that wants to make sure that you know they are the mental giant in the room, but it does seem to happen with great regularity and presumably to the delight of the brainy colossus that is overtly full of their own boastfulness.

How shall we weigh the brainiac in terms of gauging their peak-level intellectual power? I suppose you could remove their brain, place it on a scale, and see how much it weighs. Probably not very conducive though to their continuing capacity as a living, breathing, functioning human being. Speaking of physically measuring the brain, there have been all sorts of efforts to try and dig up brains of famously smart people and do various dissections of their brains, doing so in hopes of being able to ascertain what made them so sharp.

Nowadays, the usual measuring stick for figuring out someone's intellectual proficiency is the IQ (Intelligent Quotient) test.

Using a standard such as the classic Stanford-Binet Intelligence Scale test, which was first promulgated in 1916, there are often published rankings that try to make claim to whom among us is the topmost intellect. Stephen Hawking was around an IQ score of 160, something that we know due to his actually having undertaken an IQ test. Albert Einstein's score of around 160 to 190 is an estimate based on analyses of his writings and works (he apparently never took an IQ test, though he could have done so, but perhaps opted purposely to not take it or never had cause to take one).

Typically, if you can score 115 or above you are labeled as someone with high IQ. Getting a score of over 132 will get you bumped-up into the highly gifted category. The 145 and above is considered at the genius level. The highest ever recorded is supposedly a score of 263, but there is some disagreement about the matter (this score is attributed to Ainan Celeste Cawley, born in 1999 and alive to this day).

Not everyone believes in the IQ bandwagon.

Some would say that the IQ test is a questionable means to measure someone's intellectual prowess. There are predetermined aspects such as the nature of your language, your culture, and your propensity to solve puzzles, all of which makes critics decry that the IQ number is at best a surrogate of intellect and at worst a misleading gauge of intellect. There are also concerns that those that perchance score high on the IQ test will then consider themselves a kind of special class of human, perhaps encouraging them to look down upon others. The Mensa group, which is a high-IQ association, admits only those that have at least a score of 132 or other such scores depending upon the IQ test being used.

Another qualm about IQ tests is that it seems to judge your bookworm kind of thinking, more so than a true "smartness" indicator. I'm sure you've seen the common portrayal in movies and TV shows of the highly intellectual person that cannot tie their own shoes and cannot open a paper bag. If someone can do really well on tests that ask about obscure numeric patterns or mind-numbing word games, does this really showcase intellect? It might, depending upon your definition, but it generally is not considered the same as measuring your smartness.

Some believe that being smart is different than having a high intellect. You might so happen to be highly intellectual and also highly smart. There are some that believe you can be highly smart, perhaps tip top smart, and yet not necessarily have an extremely high intellect. Generally, the odds are that you'd score well on an IQ test, but the high IQ doesn't necessarily translate into being highly smart, and nor does the aspect of being highly smart necessarily indicate you'll be an A+ on an IQ test.

Another concern about any of the IQ tests is that your intellectual performance is being measured only at a given point in time. Maybe at a relatively young age you could score a quite high IQ, but later on in your middle-aged years you aren't able to score as high. Does that mean you've dropped down in your intellect? This takes us into the other word that some like to use, the word is "wisdom" and for which once again there is a debate about the relationship between wisdom, intellect, and smartness.

You might gain wisdom as you grow older, at least that's the usual expectation. Will you also increase your IQ? Some claim your IQ is your IQ, no matter what your age and when you perchance take an IQ test. This though does not bear out in terms of the reality, which is that people can take an IQ test at different points in their life and have differing scores. Plus, you can take a different kind of IQ test and score differently on it that you might on some other also "valid" IQ test.

The debate that really gets people bubbling on the IQ topic involves whether your IQ is based on nature versus nurture.

Are you born with a particular IQ level that will ultimately surface once you become of an age to be able to express it? Thus, it's a DNA kind of thing. Or, are we all perhaps born with the same IQ potential and your upbringing and environment will dictate how far your IQ will emerge? Perhaps it's a nurturing element for which some of us happen to get the proper intellectual inspirational blooming and others of us don't.

The half-in half-out answer is usually stated that you are born with some IQ capacity and it will either emerge or not depending upon your environment and how you are raised. If we put a baby in the woods to be raised by wild wolves, and the baby happened to have an IQ of 260, which we had not yet been able to measure of the tiny tot but say we guessed that the tiny baby had such an IQ, would the genius level IQ ever be showcased? Would being amongst wolves allow for the IQ to come to the surface? Would a tree make a sound if it fell in the woods and there was no one around to hear it?

Darwin had an interesting take on intellect. He proposed that your intellect might contribute toward your survivability in a manner you might not have previously considered. Sure, we would guess that if you had an IQ you could hopefully figure out how to make fire and hunt gazelles, which would presumably enhance your chances of survival. Darwin also hypothesized that topnotch intellect would attract mates and therefore boost your chance of survivability and for carrying on your legacy of high intellect.

For those of you that might have been beat-up by a strong-armed muscle rippling bully as a child, and for as much as our society seems to be keen on humans having muscular bodies, it is perhaps a surprise to consider that intellect might be so revered and be on Darwin's favorites list. We are used to the trope that the nerdish kid is the one that is physically meek and mild. The physical imposing one is the one that gets ahead and readily attracts all the mates. Our fascination with the character Spiderman is representative of this kind of imagery.

A recent study of budgerigars, a type of parrot, provides an ingenious glimpse of how we might try to test Darwin's hypothesis.

Researchers in China tried to construct an experiment to see whether female budgerigars would be more attracted to male budgerigars that demonstrated greater intellect than other male budgerigars involved in the study (this was research done by the Institute of Zoology at the Chinese Academy of Sciences in Beijing). The male budgerigars were presented with a difficult foraging task. Some were shown how to solve it, but this happened outside of the gaze of the female budgerigars.

The female budgerigars were able to watch the male participants try to open a container and access food. The males that had no prior training (i.e., not being shown the trick), were generally unable to open the container. The males that had the prior training could open the container. Presumably, the female budgerigars would infer that the males that were successful in getting the food were the intellectually sharper ones and the males that failed at doing so were intellectually inferior.

I'll steer clear for now on the question of whether this is a gender-biased study and merely note it for your noteworthiness.

In any case, the outcome of the study was that the females tended to prefer the males that had succeeded in obtaining the food from the container. You might argue that it suggests the females were more attracted to the seemingly higher intellectual males. In a manner, it provides evidence to support Darwin's hypothesis on the matter.

I realize that you are perhaps a bit skeptical about the experimental approach and whether the designed experiment really is on-target to Darwin's theory.

For example, how do we know what the female budgerigars were really thinking about? Maybe they ascribed other attributes to the males that succeeded in the task, and those attributes might have little or nothing to do with a perceived sense of intellectual prowess.

Furthermore, the females were never allowed to try and undertake the task, so they were not fully aware of what the task consisted of and had to base their "choices" as to the males based solely on watching them perform the experimental task.

Another potential weakness about the study involves our overall conundrum about how to measure intellect. The means of figuring out how to get into a locked container might be considered a problem-solving kind of task, which might or might not require high intellect, and therefore we could debate if intellect is truly being encompassed and exhibited in this study. Were the males merely showcasing keen problem-solving skills rather than high intellect per se?

Based on the experimental design, we need to accept the idea that we are to infer that the container access matter is a sign of good problem solving and that correspondingly a good problem solver is ergo a high intellectual. Recall that earlier it was pointed out that smartness and intellect are not necessarily the same. Why should we believe that keen problem-solving and intellect are necessarily the same? They probably are not, most would likely say.

Is this problem-solving task a valid surrogate in lieu of administering to the budgerigars our now-accepted IQ measurement tool, namely the Stanford-Binet Intelligence Scale test? Makes one kind of chuckle to consider how we might get the budgerigars to take a conventional IQ test. Ponder, how might we ask these Australian parakeets to take an IQ test. These gregarious parakeets are typically referred to as the budgie, and I'd suggest it would be quite interesting to watch as the budgie "read" a conventional IQ test and pencil in, or shall we say peck in, their answers.

Let's get back to human intellect. The parakeet study was mainly to illuminate that intellect is presumably a quite important matter and that Darwin was a proponent of the belief that intellect ties to survivability, doing so for humans and other animals too.

In the field of Artificial Intelligence (AI), the presumed overarching goal consists of trying to make machines that seem to exhibit the equivalent of human intelligence.

I've tried to word that sentence carefully. Notice that I'm saying that the machine is not necessarily the same as humans in terms of how human intelligence exists. Many would assert that if we can reach intelligence in machines and do so in a manner that might be quite different than how humans arise to intelligence, we have nonetheless succeeded in achieving artificial intelligence.

The famous Turing Test is a somewhat simple notion of how we might measure whether AI has been achieved or not. Generally, it consists of having a machine that has presumably AI that competes with a human that presumably has human intelligence, and another human asks questions of the two competitors. If the human inquisitor cannot differentiate between the two competitors and is unable to state which is the AI and which is the human, one could infer that the AI has achieved human intelligence.

Here's a good question to contemplate. How high is up?

I mention this because the question arises as to how much intelligence do we need to say that there is an AI that is indeed intelligent? Suppose an AI system can pass the Turing Test. Suppose further we give the AI an IQ test. Many would claim that a score of 70 or lower is an indicator of an intellectual disability. Imagine what we would be pondering if the AI took an IQ test and got a score of say 50.

What a dilemma! We have an AI system that appeared to pass the Turing Test and seems to be intelligent, and yet at the same time did quite poorly on the IQ test. I realize you might assert that the AI would have been unable to succeed at the Turing Test if it did not have a sufficient IQ, presumably an IQ of at least around 100, which is the "normal" average that usually is scored. I'm not so convinced that you are correct in that assertion.

I'll shift our attention though from the bottom side of the IQ scale to the top side of the IQ scale. How high up will we want the AI to score? If the AI can score at say 115, which is the considered high-IQ range, would that be sufficient?

Consider this scenario. Your life is in the hands of a robot that must decide what to do and potentially save you. You can choose a robot that has an IQ of 50 (considered intellectually disabled), or one that has an IQ of 100 (intellectually average for a human), or one that has a score of 115 (high IQ), or a score of 160 (Stephen Hawking's score), or 190 (exceeds genius), or even let's say the never-yet-human achieved score of 300 (knocking the socks off the IQ test!).

I'm guessing you'll pick the highest possible number.

You would presumably use the logic that the higher the intellect of the robot then the greater the chance of it making sure your life is saved. Why take a chance on a robot that has "only" an IQ of 160 (Hawking's level and Einstein's level), if you could pick one that is off-the-charts at 300? If you could get yourself a robot that had the AI equivalence of two-times the score of Einstein, it would seem unwise of you to take anything lower.

Right now, AI systems are being built and deployed, but there isn't anyone especially measuring what their intellectual score is. The belief seems to be that if the AI can "do the job" it was intended to do, hopefully it is intellectually commemorate enough. Should we be pleased with this approach? Are you willing to be at the mercy of an AI system for which no one even knows how intellectually low or high it is?

We also need to revisit the earlier points about smartness versus intellect. I can tell you straight out that the AI of today does not have smartness. The AI of today is brittle and considered narrow and lacks what often is referred to as Artificial General Intelligence (AGI).

I also earlier mentioned the notion of wisdom, which, again the AI of today would be far below any kind of wisdom scale (not even anywhere on such a scale). There are ongoing efforts to try and imbue AI with common sense reasoning, but it is a long slow road, and nobody knows whether it will ever even succeed.

What does this have to do with AI self-driving cars?

At the Cybernetic AI Self-Driving Car Institute, we are developing AI software for self-driving cars. One question that nobody seems to yet be asking is whether or not we are supposed to be aiming for regular cognition or something more pronounced such as superior cognition. This ties to the discussion herein so far about intellect.

Allow me to elaborate.

I'd like to first clarify and introduce the notion that there are varying levels of AI self-driving cars. The topmost level is considered Level 5. A Level 5 self-driving car is one that is being driven by the AI and there is no human driver involved. For the design of Level 5 self-driving cars, the auto makers are even removing the gas pedal, brake pedal, and steering wheel, since those are contraptions used by human drivers. The Level 5 self-driving car is not being driven by a human and nor is there an expectation that a human driver will be present in the self-driving car. It's all on the shoulders of the AI to drive the car.

For self-driving cars less than a Level 5, there must be a human driver present in the car. The human driver is currently considered the responsible party for the acts of the car. The AI and the human driver are co-sharing the driving task. In spite of this co-sharing, the human is supposed to remain fully immersed into the driving task and be ready at all times to perform the driving task. I've repeatedly warned about the dangers of this co-sharing arrangement and predicted it will produce many untoward results.

Let's focus herein on the true Level 5 self-driving car. Much of the comments apply to the less than Level 5 self-driving cars too, but the fully autonomous AI self-driving car will receive the most attention in this discussion.

Here's the usual steps involved in the AI driving task:

- Sensor data collection and interpretation
- Sensor fusion
- Virtual world model updating
- AI action planning
- Car controls command issuance

Another key aspect of AI self-driving cars is that they will be driving on our roadways in the midst of human driven cars too. There are some pundits of AI self-driving cars that continually refer to a utopian world in which there are only AI self-driving cars on the public roads. Currently there are about 250+ million conventional cars in the United States alone, and those cars are not going to magically disappear or become true Level 5 AI self-driving cars overnight.

Indeed, the use of human driven cars will last for many years, likely many decades, and the advent of AI self-driving cars will occur while there are still human driven cars on the roads. This is a crucial point since this means that the AI of self-driving cars needs to be able to contend with not just other AI self-driving cars, but also contend with human driven cars. It is easy to envision a simplistic and rather unrealistic world in which all AI self-driving cars are politely interacting with each other and being civil about roadway interactions. That's not what is going to be happening for the foreseeable future. AI self-driving cars and human driven cars will need to be able to cope with each other.

Returning to the topic of cognition and intellect, let's consider how the matter of the level of intellect applies to the advent of AI self-driving cars.

We've so far considered whether there is a need to aim for a "highest feasible" intellect for an AI system that we might be constructing and fielding. For AI that is designed and built to drive a car, what level of intellectual prowess should be the overarching goal?

First, you could say that we should aim at the level of intellect as exhibited by humans in the case of performing the driving task. That would seem to be a reasonable marker as to the intellect that we as a society expect for execution of driving a car.

In that case, you would be hard pressed to suggest that any kind of "higher" intellect is needed per se. Generally, the average person is able to obtain a driver's license and legally be able to drive a car. As such, we'd presumably say that an "average" IQ is sufficient for the driving effort, and therefore we could be satisfied with an average IQ in terms of the AI that would be driving a car. Perhaps a score of around 100 would be satisfactory.

Suppose we pushed to get the AI of a self-driving car to a higher level of IQ. Would we gain much?

It is not especially convincing that a higher intellect is going to make that much difference in undertaking the driving task. Are expert-level drivers that race cars of a higher intellect? There doesn't seem to be much study on that matter, but I'd guess that those race car drivers are more versed in the driving of cars and yet are not intellectually especially at a higher level than the rest of us. Are professional drivers such as cabbies or truck drivers at a higher level of intellect than average car drivers? Again, there doesn't seem to be much evidence to suggest they are.

If we don't seem to have a base of high intellects that drive cars, in other words no set of high IQ's that happen to drive cars and that have been studied to see whether they are somehow more proficient at driving cars, we are left to speculate about the higher IQ and its relationship to driving. You could claim that a higher intellect might be able to more rapidly think when driving a car and be able to mentally add something to the driving chore.

Perhaps a higher intellect would allow a human driver to be more adept at piecing together the clues of the driving scene.

They might be able to see that there is a car up ahead and that there is a pedestrian on the sidewalk, and be able to put together puzzle pieces in a manner that lets them know the odds are that the car is going to hit its brakes, due to the pedestrian likely stepping onto the street, which will then cause the cars behind the stopped car to come to a sudden halt, and will cascade into a potential car crash. Notably, all of these mentally complex calculations being undertaken in a fraction of second, faster and more completely than someone of a lesser but average intellect.

In that manner, a higher intellect might foster being able to envision more complex car-related traffic possibilities. A higher intellect might enable the driver to find clues about the driving situation that those of an average intellect would fail to piece together. A higher intellect might suggest that the driver would be faster at processing the driving situation. This faster mental processing might allow for being able to sooner avoid adverse driving moments.

Whereas an average driver might get "caught off-guard" because of not having detective-like realized the clues of a pending driving problem, a higher intellect might be more likely to do so. And by mentally processing it faster, this gives the higher intellect driver more available options since they sooner ascertained that some driving action was needed, upping the chances of being able to select among more early escape options.

I realize you might argue that perhaps the higher intellect is not necessarily going to get all of those driving advantages. Similar to the study of the budgerigars, perhaps driving a car is a problem-solving task and not as influenced simply by having higher intellect. You could assert that being able to perceive a driving scene and make life-critical decisions about operating a car is more so a problem-solving task rather than a purely intellectual exercise.

Thus, we might be barking up a wrong tree by trying to lay claim that the higher intellect will ergo lead to being a more adept driver. The higher intellect might allow someone to be a better or faster problem-solver, but this is not axiomatic. These are two different items, whether being a topnotch problem solver versus having a high intellect. Presumably, if a higher intellect wanted to be a topnotch problem solver, they might have an easier time of doing so, prodded on by their high intellect, though it is not automatically the case.

We can also wonder whether a higher intellect might actually work against the notion of being a better driver of a car.

Remember the earlier mention that we as a society seem to assume that the higher intellect is often in the clouds in terms of not paying attention to day-to-day elements of life. We portray high intellects as unable to tie their own shoes. If that's the case, it would seem that suggesting they are going to be driving a car at a higher plateau of driving proficiency is actually the opposite of what we should expect. We apparently should be worried about these higher intellects driving a car. They might be less able to do so in comparison to an average intellect driver.

Why would it be the case that a higher intellect might be a poorer or worse driver than someone of an average IQ?

You might at first assume that certainly the higher intellect would win at any task involving intellectual effort. The physical aspects of driving are generally rather simplistic, involving pushing a brake pedal and an accelerator pedal, and steering a wheel, all of which even a very young child can do. It's the intellectual aspects of driving a car that appear to make the difference of being a proficient driver versus one that is not so proficient. A driver that cannot think quickly enough and tie together their sensory clues is one that is seemingly more likely to get into car accidents and create untoward traffic conditions.

We already as a society are concerned about distracted drivers. A distracted driver is one that is not paying attention to the driving task. The distraction can involve a physical form of distraction, such as taking your hands off the wheel to manipulate your smartphone, or maybe turning your head to talk to someone in the backseat of the car and thus your head is now turned away from the driving scene. The distraction can also be a form of intellectual distraction.

When your mind is focused on a text that you have just read on your smartphone, you are no longer well-engaged in the driving task. Even if your head and eyes are now facing the roadway, your mental awareness of the traffic conditions is going to be weakened by your mental preoccupation about the text that you read. I know that there is a lot of concern about using a smartphone while driving, but we've already had other forms of mental distractions too, such as talking with others in your car and discussing say the latest in politics or some other non-driving related matter.

You don't even necessarily need to have something prompt you to mentally become disengaged with the driving task. Have you ever caught yourself daydreaming while driving your car? Imagine you are driving from Los Angeles to San Francisco, a six hour or so drive, and suppose it is a quiet traffic day and the main highway is pretty much empty. Nothing but miles upon miles of farms and rolling hills. For some people, they find themselves unable to concentrate on the roadway and their minds wander. This lack of mental connection to the driving task can catch them unaware if suddenly a tire blows or a deer darts across the highway.

One could suggest that at higher level of intellect you might be able to multi-task mentally more so than someone of an average intellect. If that's the case, perhaps a minor mental distraction would not materially impact your driving, while for the person of average intellect it could have a more pronounced impact. In essence, if we imagine that intellect is like an apple pie, thinking about some text that you just got might consume half of the apple pie for an average intellect, but only a tiny slice of the apple pie of the higher intellect.

On the other hand, one could claim that perhaps the greater intellect is more prone to tossing their intellect at everything that comes along. In that case, whereas the average intellect might devote just a small mental slice to consider the text they just received, it could be that the higher intellect pours all of their mental capacity into thinking about the text, therefore having very limited intellect leftover to focus on the driving task.

I had earlier indicated that we often say that someone is smarter than their britches or too smart for their own good. If we reword this to suggest that someone has too high an intellect for their own good, let's see how that might impact their intellectual prowess and see how it could impact their driving.

I'll consider these five exemplars of the potential adverse consequences of high intellect:

- Analysis Paralysis

- Dismissiveness

- Shallowness of Thought

- Over-Thinking

- False Over-Confidence

Analysis Paralysis.

A higher intellect might be more prone to analyzing a myriad of options. Will that car ahead opt to make a sudden lane change? Will the pedestrian leap into the street? Is that traffic light going to change to red in the next few seconds? All of this thinking can produce analysis paralysis. The driver becomes preoccupied with analyzing what to do or what might happen, and as a result they aren't making the kinds of rapid decisions that need to be made when driving a car.

Dismissiveness.

A higher intellect might be dismissive of others. You've likely had someone that thinks they are so sharp that they dismiss other people's ideas or suggestions. Unless they believe the other person is of an equal intellect, they don't get much credence to the other person. A driver that is dismissiveness might opt to ignore a warning from a front seat passenger that tells them a car to their right is possibly going to intervene into their lane. This dismissiveness can undermine the driving effort.

Shallowness of Thought.

A higher intellect often will categorize mental tasks and then proclaim that a particular task is not worthy of their intellectual powers. As a driver, a higher intellect might be tempted to consider the driving task as menial. As a result, the person is unwilling to put much mental effort toward driving. They prefer to operate a car with a shallowness of thought. If they do so, it could spell danger as they are potentially underestimating what they need to be considering in order to be a safe driver.

Over-Thinking.

A higher intellect might tend toward over-thinking every moment of the driving task. I knew someone that was looking at every angle at every step of driving a car. They made incredible mental leaps about the aspects that could go awry, almost to the degree that they even were calculating the chances of a meteor striking the earth in front of their car. This over-thinking can cause them to become muddled and overwhelmed about the driving task.

False Over-Confidence.

A higher intellect might believe that they are the best driver ever, which is fueled by their belief in their own astounding intellect. This leads to over-confidence. They assume that for any driving situation they will be able to mentally find a means of driving the car to escape. This type of driver can be riskier in their driving and get themselves into binds that they are actually unable to get out of safely.

I am not saying that only higher intellects will potentially fall victim to the aforementioned mental guffaws. Any driver can suffer from analysis paralysis, and from dismissiveness, and from shallowness of thought, and from over-thinking, and from false over-confidence. I'd bet though that the higher intellect is perhaps more likely to find themselves falling into these traps. It is the basis for why we have as a society come up with the too smart for their own britches label.

Could an AI system for a self-driving car also be vulnerable to these same kinds of mental underpinnings?

Sure, each of these intellectual dangers can readily happen to an AI system. I don't want you to though assume I am saying that AI is sentient, and it is succumbing to these mental impairments in the same manner that a human might. I am not suggesting or implying this.

Instead, I am trying to assert that the AI as a form of automation can suffer the same deficiencies and it is up to the AI developers to try and make sure that the AI is not caught off-guard by these computationally equivalent mental maladies.

For example, analysis paralysis can befall the AI if it gets bogged down trying to explore a large search space and fails to realize that time is crucial to making a driving decision. The AI could be so engrossed in assessing the sensory data and the virtual world model that it lets the clock continue to run. The running clock means that the world outside the self-driving car is moving and changing, which might mean that the AI is gradually losing out on options for making a vital car driving decision.

I had predicted that the Uber incident in Arizona might partially have occurred because of the time taken by the AI to try and assess the driving situation. Preliminary reports assessing the Uber incident appeared to have echoed that point. Though some might shrug their shoulders and say that's just the way the real-time automation works, I am not one to fall into the trap of allowing automation to be some kind of independent amorphous entity that happens to do what it does. I hold accountable the AI developers that should be developing their AI systems to handle these kinds of real-time situations.

Conclusion

Is superior cognition needed to drive a car? We might debate the meaning of the word "superior" and be at odds about the notion of what being superior in cognition consists of.

If we use the everyday notion of IQ, the question can be rephrased as to whether higher IQ is needed to drive a car. There seems little evidence to suggest that any particular level of above average IQ is a needed element to drive a car, since the world at large appears to be able to drive a car and we can reasonably assume therefore it involves an average IQ effort.

It could be that if we can achieve AI that can drive a self-driving car, we might want to see what it can do if it is pushed to a higher level of intellect. Perhaps we might have better driving and safer driving. This is not though necessarily the case. We also need to be aware of the kinds of mental maladies that seem to at times correspond to having higher intellect, and whether those might be found in AI systems and therefore undermine the heightened intellect aspects.

I've not entertained herein the conspiracy theorists that are worried that we might be pushing the AI intellect to a point that it surpasses human intellect and then opts to take over humanity. The paperclip making super-intelligence mankind-overtaking AI I've covered elsewhere. For now, I'm merely trying to get AI developers to consider the degree of intellect that they are aiming to achieve in their AI systems, and also prodding the rest of us to also consider what level of intellect are we becoming vulnerable to in terms of AI systems that increasingly are entering into our lives.

I've highlighted the nature of AI self-driving cars as a key indicator of how the intellect might come to play. Many AI systems are not as involved in making immediate life-or-death decision as those of AI self-driving cars.

I would hope that we would be more concerned about the intellect prowess of AI systems that are in the role of deciding whether a multi-ton car is going to make that right turn or maybe come to a sudden stop, all of which the lives of humans hang in the balance. It sure seems like having superior cognition would be a handy capability, if properly designed and deployed. The Einstein AI for self-driving cars has kind of a ring to it, doesn't it.

CHAPTER 8
AMALGAMATING ODD'S
AND
AI SELF-DRIVING CARS

CHAPTER 8

AMALGAMATING ODD'S
AND
AI SELF-DRIVING CARS

When I got my very first car, I was so excited to be driving my own car that I opted to drive everywhere that I could think of.

I drove all throughout my local neighborhood and honked my horn as I drove past the homes of friends of mine. I drove beyond my community and took the freeway to go visit friends that lived in the inner-city areas. I drove down to the beach, parked at the edge of the sand, and took a picture of me and my car, including as a backdrop a dramatic sunset and the rays of the sun glinting off the ocean, adding a picturesque look to my shiny new automobile.

The next day, I took some friends up to the snowy mountains. I had made sure to buy snow-chains for my tires and it was my first foray into putting them on and seeing how the car handled on icy roads and in light snowy conditions. I kept on the snow-plowed roads and did not venture into any off-roading, since my car was, well, just a regular car, and I figured it would be quite a risk to see if it could cope with off-road adversities.

Upon returning from the mountains, a good friend suggested we head out to the desert. The mountain trip had involved freezing cold temperatures. Perhaps by going to the dry and hot desert, we'd be able to unfreeze and gain back our normal body temp. With my still brand-new car, we drove on a somewhat barren highway and headed out to the middle of the desert. Once we reached the outskirts of the desert, we went off the main highway and took roads that were only sporadically paved. At one point, we were driving on dirt-like sand-packed roads. I came to a stop before we ended-up in an actual loose desert sand.

Not being content with "only" having driven in the city, the suburbs, the mountains, and the desert, I decided that the next adventure with my car would be to the forest. So, I packed my camping gear into the car and drove up to the redwoods. I was able to get a campground that allowed you to park your car right next to where you were going to put your tent. Today, some would say this is a form of glamping, a somewhat newer word that means camping with luxury. Admittedly, being right next to my car was handy and a reassurance.

Imagine my horror if a bear were to have tried to pry into my car to get the food I had brought – I would have been devastated that my new car got banged up by the evil claws!

As I headed back home, the forest got deluged with quite a rainstorm. Driving out of the woods was a bit tricky as some of the roads began to flood. I was lucky that the rain was only drenching the roads and not completely flooding them. I inched my way out of the woods on the paved roads that were wet and at times I worried that the car might get too much water up into the engine compartment.

One other thing that I encountered was a lot of potholes and other marred roadway aspects. Because of the rain on the road, I was not able to readily discern where the cracks and gaps in the asphalt existed. Normally, I would have tried to steer around any potholes or other street maladies. In this case, I opted to focus on staying on the road and not sliding off the road, thus, if I happened to also hit any bumps or holes in the road, so be it, at least I was still on the road itself.

In the initial two weeks of getting my first car, I likely put as many miles on it as some people do in an entire year. I'd wager that most young people are equally excited when they get their first car. It is a means to have mobility. You can go where you want. You can go when you want. Previously, prior to getting my own car, I had to borrow my parents car or see if I could get a friend to use their car or loan me their car for any driving trips I wanted to make. Now, I instead just walked out to my car, put the key in the ignition, and by gosh I could go wherever I pleased. Yippee!

There were of course some limits about where I could drive. My car was not suited to doing off-roading. I realized that I could either wreck my new car or get stuck if I tried to go off-road. But, nonetheless, I pushed that limit quite a bit. My driving out to the desert got me and my beloved car pretty close to being off-road. When I drove to the beach, it was at the edge of off-road once I touched the sandy beaches. At the woods, and up in the snowy mountains, I pretty much put my on-road-only car into situations that were darned close to an off-road journey.

The limits I had in mind were all based on what the car could and could not do. Though I was still a rather young and inexperienced driver, it didn't occur to me that my ability to drive the car ought to be another form of limitation.

I sheepishly admit that during the snowy mountain trip, I lost control of the car and it skidded into a snow bank. My fault. I was not driving carefully enough for the snowy conditions and also had never particular practiced at driving in such conditions. While driving out of the forest, I got caught in semi-flooded roads. I had never driven a car in rain-soaked situations. I managed to get out of the woods without injury, though other cars around me were certainly wary of my swerving and inexperienced efforts of driving the car.

You could say that driving a car involves various potential limits. One obvious limit is the capability of the car. I had a colleague that never drove his car up to the mountains. Why, you might ask? He insisted that the engine was on its last legs and the strain to drive up steep roads would wipe it out. He even avoided driving on any high inclines in city driving, making sure to take the long way around if he could avoid streets that were at a steep pitch.

I was willing to take my new car just about anywhere that a road existed. I trusted that since it was a new car, it would be able to handle high speeds, low speeds, bumpy roads, smooth roads, highways, freeways, and the rest. According to the Federal Highway Administration (FHA), there are slightly more than four million miles of roads in the United States. I was determined to see if I could drive everyone of those many millions of miles in my nifty new car. That hope was a bit challenging since the four million miles includes Hawaii and Alaska, which would take some doing to reach.

The driver of a car is certainly another limitation.

Some drivers are not versed in driving in snowy conditions. Unless they really needed to drive in such inclement conditions, such as in a dire emergency, it's probably best if they didn't venture into situations involving driving in the snow (until they got some training in doing so).

Here in Southern California, it is a standard joke that most drivers do not seem to be able to drive in the rain. We got so little rain that one might generously suggest we are out of practice of rain driving. When I have visitors from other parts of the country where they routinely get rain and must drive in it, they scoff and laugh at the manner of how locals here drive in the rain. In any case, one could say that a driver that is not versed in rain driving is another kind of limitation related to the driving of a car.

In the official parlance of the automotive industry, the way in which you can define the scope and limits of driving are referred to as a "domain" and commonly indicated as the Operational Design Domain (ODD). Per the IEEE standard known as J3016, here's what ODD formally means: "… operating conditions under which a given driving automation system or feature thereof is specifically designed to function, including, but not limited to, environmental, geographical, and time-of-day restrictions, and/or the requisite presence or absence of certain traffic or roadway characteristics."

That's a bit of a mouthful.

In essence, an ODD is a kind of carve out. Imagine all of the numerous ways in which driving might occur such as in fine weather or bad weather, on bumpy roads or smooth roads, and so on. In that universe of a myriad of driving conditions, you can stake out a subset and declare it to be an ODD.

For example, I might define an ODD that consists of smooth roads, absence of rain and the roads must be dry, and there must be high visibility in terms of being able to see around the car. That's my declared ODD. It's just one such ODD. I might define a second ODD, for which it consists of smooth and bumpy roads, light rain allowed, roads can be wet but not slick, and the visibility can range from high to mediocre.

I could continue declaring various ODDs. Each of the ODDs would have some particular set of indicators about what it includes. This might also include exclusions, thus I can probably be clearer about my ODDs by not only saying what it includes but also what it excludes. That being said, the number of exclusions could be rather vast and perhaps exhausting to try and list them all.

There is no accepted standard as to what the ODDs are.

Anyone can make-up their own ODDs.

I've provided you with two ODDs that I just made-up. You might decide that you like those ODDs and opt to use the same ones, exactly as I had declared them, offering no changes or adjustments to them.

Or, maybe you decide to make a variant of my ODDs. For the first ODD that I declared, you decide to add that the roads cannot include any roundabouts or traffic circles. I didn't state in my ODD whether or not roundabouts were allowed, but you could likely assume that since I had not said it was excluded, it presumably was included.

You now are making sure to explicitly state that roundabouts are excluded. In that case, my ODD and your ODD are now different from each other.

Think of the number and variety of ODDs that could be declared. By mixing and matching all permutations and combinations of the myriad of factors, you could create an enormous number of ODDs. Besides the roadway aspects, you can state that an ODD is good for daylight but does not encompass night time. Thus, time of day can be a factor. The geographical area can be a factor, such as I might declare my first ODD was intended only for say Los Angeles and no other geographical realm.

On and on this can go.

Who would be making up these ODDs? The auto makers can do so and will likely need to do so. They aren't the only ones and it is pretty much a free-for-all as to whom can declare ODDs. Researchers can make them up. Industry analysts can make them up. You and I can make them up.

I suppose you might be thinking it seems like a rather hazy thing and kind of loose. Yes, you'd be right about that. You might also be thinking that this ODD is something you've not heard about before and therefore it doesn't seem to matter much. I'd say you are half-right about that.

ODDs are indeed something you've had no cause to necessarily hear about or know about, to-date. But, I fully and boldly predict that pretty soon you'll be hearing all about them. A lot. It will become a big topic. You will likely ultimately become so familiar with ODDs that you will forget that you ever didn't know about them. That's how prevalent awareness of ODDs is going to become.

What does this have to do with AI self-driving cars?

At the Cybernetic AI Self-Driving Car Institute, we are developing AI software for self-driving cars. For the Level 4 and Level 5 of AI self-driving cars, the nature and use of ODDs is essential. Once the public begins to experience Level 4 and Level 5 AI self-driving cars on the roadways, the ODDs topic is going to hit the big time and be at the forefront of public discussion and discord. Mark my words!

Allow me to elaborate.

I'd like to first clarify and introduce the notion that there are varying levels of AI self-driving cars. The topmost level is considered Level 5. A Level 5 self-driving car is one that is being driven by the AI and there is no human driver involved. For the design of Level 5 self-driving cars, the auto makers are even removing the gas pedal, brake pedal, and steering wheel, since those are contraptions used by human drivers. The Level 5 self-driving car is not being driven by a human and nor is there an expectation that a human driver will be present in the self-driving car. It's all on the shoulders of the AI to drive the car.

For self-driving cars less than a Level 5, there must be a human driver present in the car. The human driver is currently considered the responsible party for the acts of the car. The AI and the human driver are co-sharing the driving task. In spite of this co-sharing, the human is supposed to remain fully immersed into the driving task and be ready at all times to perform the driving task. I've repeatedly warned about the dangers of this co-sharing arrangement and predicted it will produce many untoward results.

Let's focus herein on the true Level 5 self-driving car. Much of the comments apply to the less than Level 5 self-driving cars too, but the fully autonomous AI self-driving car will receive the most attention in this discussion.

Here's the usual steps involved in the AI driving task:

- Sensor data collection and interpretation
- Sensor fusion
- Virtual world model updating
- AI action planning
- Car controls command issuance

Another key aspect of AI self-driving cars is that they will be driving on our roadways in the midst of human driven cars too. There are some pundits of AI self-driving cars that continually refer to a utopian world in which there are only AI self-driving cars on the public roads. Currently there are about 250+ million conventional cars in the United States alone, and those cars are not going to magically disappear or become true Level 5 AI self-driving cars overnight.

Indeed, the use of human driven cars will last for many years, likely many decades, and the advent of AI self-driving cars will occur while there are still human driven cars on the roads. This is a crucial point since this means that the AI of self-driving cars needs to be able to contend with not just other AI self-driving cars, but also contend with human driven cars. It is easy to envision a simplistic and rather unrealistic world in which all AI self-driving cars are politely interacting with each other and being civil about roadway interactions. That's not what is going to be happening for the foreseeable future. AI self-driving cars and human driven cars will need to be able to cope with each other.

Returning to the topic of ODDs, let's take a closer look at what they are and why they are going to be so crucial to the advent of AI self-driving cars.

Level 4 self-driving cars must provide an indication of the ODDs under which they are able to operate.

This means that if you are intending to purchase a Level 4 self-driving car, you would be wise to look carefully at the ODDs that the auto maker says are applicable to the automobile you are about to purchase. You would likely give this even more scrutiny than the typical features of a car such as the Miles Per Gallon (MPG) or how many cup holders it has.

The reason to scrutinize the ODDs is so that you'll then know where, when, and under what circumstances your AI self-driving car is going to be able to operate as a self-driving car. According the standard definition for Level 4, once the AI detects that it has reached a point that the driving is no longer within its defined ODDs, the AI is supposed to let the human driver in the car take over or the AI is supposed to pull over, finding hopefully a safe spot to do so, and wait to continue driving until the situation becomes one encompassed by the ODDs of that particular AI self-driving car.

Let's suppose you buy an AI self-driving car that has a bunch of ODDs and in addition mentions various exclusions of aspects that fall outside of those ODDs. Pretend that one of the exclusions is that the AI self-driving car will not drive in snowy conditions. You would need to dig deeper into how the particular auto maker is defining snowy conditions such as whether this includes a light dusting of fully snowflakes or maybe it only counts once a heavy snowstorm erupts and dumps a ton of snow onto the roadway.

In any case, there you are, going along for a spin in your fancy new Level 4 AI self-driving car. It is a wintery day. When you began your joyful journey, the skies were relatively barren of clouds. Sure, it was a cold morning as you got underway, but you didn't expect bad weather to occur. Darned if toward lunch time, clouds started coming in fast. With the cold temperatures and the clouds forming, it begins to snow.

The AI of the Level 4 self-driving car is presumably able to detect the snowfall, doing so via the sensors of the self-driving car. Because the ODDs indicated the AI is not considered able to drive in snowy conditions, the AI alerts you that you'll need to take over the driving of the self-driving car. If you refuse or don't speak-up, the default will be to pull the self-driving car over to the side of the road at the earliest feasible and hopefully safe spot.

Even though you might be able to drive the self-driving car, and you are willing to do in spite of the flakes of snow, and there's lots of other car traffic around you that is doing so, your AI is not going to budge one inch. The ODD boundaries have been reached. You would need to take the controls if you didn't want to sit there by the side of the road and wait for whenever next the snow cleared up sufficiently that the AI declared it was okay for it to proceed and would continue on the driving journey.

I realize you might say that it is a small inconvenience in this case. No big deal, you say, it's a minor annoyance that the AI has opted to no longer drive the self-driving car for the moment. For your driving journey, at least it drove you for a substantial part of the time. You can just now take over the driving and finish the trip. Furthermore, if you are able to drive out of the snowy area, you likely can coax the AI to resume driving the self-driving car.

But, imagine that you decided to have your Level 4 AI self-driving car take the kids to school that morning. You had put the kids into the self-driving car and sternly instructed the AI to drive them straight to the school. It had done this many times before.

Unfortunately, on this particular day, let's assume that the snow starts to fall from the sky while midway to the school. The AI announces that it needs either a licensed driver to take over the controls right away or it will pull over to the side of the road. There isn't a licensed driver in the self-driving car (you are still at home, awaiting the self-driving car to drop the kids at their school and come back to pick you up to drive you to work). Only your underage children are in the self-driving car. They can't legally drive and nor do they know how to drive.

Regrettably, they now are going to be sitting in the dormant and roadway parked AI self-driving car which has found hopefully a safe place to sit out the snow. For most parents, this would be a chilling moment and the time at which they start to have second-thoughts about having gotten that Level 4 AI self-driving car.

You could say that the parent was "foolish" for having put the children into the AI self-driving car without any adult present. I assure you this is exactly what many, if not most parents are going to do. They are going to leverage the always-available automated chauffeur. It will become more than just a handy convenience. Parents will adjust their lives around the aspect that they no longer need to drive their children to all sorts of places, such as no need to drive your children to school, nor to baseball practice, nor to karate lessons, nor to the local pizza place.

You might say that the parent should have known it was going to snow. In that case, on this occasion, the parent should have gone along for the ride, serving as a "human back-up" driver in case the AI had to call it quits. Yes, I suppose you could try to take that angle on this scenario, but I hope that you won't get quite so literal on this one example.

My overall point is that the ODD's of the Level 4 AI self-driving car could consist of a wide variety of inclusions and exclusions. I made things over-simplified by using just the snowy condition. There might instead by a large number of inclusions and exclusions, making it much harder to judge when you might have the AI opt to quit on you. It won't be so easy that you'll readily be able to predict when the exclusions are going to be reached.

I also made things easier by suggesting you had chosen to buy the Level 4 AI self-driving car. I say that's "easier" because you presumably would have carefully read the ODDs before you purchased that self-driving car.

You would have done your due diligence and fully understood what the various inclusions and exclusions consist of. You would have tried to identify the ways in which you'll be using the self-driving car, such as the geographical area you live in, the seasons of the year, and other factors, all of which would have led you to via full-awareness having decided to buy that self-driving car.

At least that's what should happen, though we know that people don't necessarily take that kind of overt care and caution when buying a car.

The other way in which the ODDs will impact you is when you use a ridesharing service.

It is predicted that ridesharing services will flock in droves to using AI self-driving cars. This makes a lot of sense for the ridesharing firms to do so. No need to deal with a human driver for their ridesharing cars. Human drivers are difficult, because they are humans, which means they want to get paid for their driving, they want reasonable hours of driving time, they want to take breaks periodically, and so on. With an AI system, no need to deal with any of those human elements.

You are getting off work early and decide to take a ridesharing car to get home. Via a mobile app on your smartphone, you summon a ridesharing car, doing so with a company that prides itself on providing all and only AI self-driving cars. They are using Level 4 AI self-driving cars. One handy aspect is that the company keeps those AI self-driving cars going as much as possible, running them nearly non-stop 24x7, other than when the self-driving cars need to get their electrical charges or when they are out for maintenance purposes.

A few minutes later, the AI self-driving car comes to the curb and you get into it. You had already indicated your destination and thus the AI repeats to you the destination, confirming where you want to go, and once you get settled with your seatbelt on, the AI proceeds. How nice that you don't need to carry on petty conversations with those pesky human ridesharing drivers. The AI tries to initiate a dialogue with you, but you cut it off and state that you want a nice quiet ride instead. No need to worry about hurting the feelings of the AI. It's just AI.

Unbeknownst to you, this particular Level 4 AI self-driving car has an ODD that the auto maker and tech firm defined to exclude heavy gusts of winds. Your home is nestled in a rural area where you thought it would be best to raise a family. The drive from work, which is downtown, and out to the rural area usually takes about an hour or so. On this day, there is a strong set of winds blowing along the highway that takes you to your home.

While on the highway, you can see up ahead that the winds are shoving trucks and other cars. It is occurring with some frequency. There doesn't seem to be any problems though and the vehicles are all continuing along on the blustery highway. You begin to take a nap in the backseat, enjoying the ridesharing ride that lets you take it easy because the AI is doing the driving.

All of a sudden, the AI announces that you will need to take over the driving or it will be pulling over to the side of the road momentarily. Why, you ask? The AI responds that the wind speeds are excessive and exceed the defined ODD for this AI self-driving car. Yikes! You had no idea that this ridesharing car had that kind of an ODD. You are irked to no end.

I realize that you might object to my scenario and say that the ridesharing service should have informed the rider about the ODDs. Yes, I am sure that the ridesharing services will post the ODD's of their cars. When you book one of their cars, there will likely be a place to click on a lengthy legal-looking narrative that carefully spells out all of the inclusions and exclusions. I wonder how many people will go to the trouble to read those? Probably the same number that read the legal limits and caveats that the ridesharing services also post at their sites right now (have you ever read those?).

If you are assuming that this ODD matter is going to be simplified by merely having all AI self-driving cars adopt the same ODDs, I'll remind you that I earlier had stated that there is no such standard.

This means that if you consider buying a Level 4 AI self-driving car from auto maker X, they will presumably have defined whatever set of ODDs they wanted to establish for their Level 4 AI self-driving cars. They might also have different sets of ODDs among their own line of Level 4 AI self-driving cars.

Maybe the low-end lower-cost Level 4 AI self-driving car of auto maker X has one set of ODDs, we'll call it the AI-1 model, while their more expensive higher-end Level 4 AI self-driving car has a more extensive set of ODDs, we'll call it the AI-2 model. When you buy the car, you'll need to decide whether you are fine with the lesser set of ODDs and buy the AI-1 or might get stuck at some point and so prefer to get the more in-depth set of ODDs offered by the AI-2.

Furthermore, keep in mind that another auto maker, we'll call them auto maker Y, they are able to define their own ODDs. You might not be able to readily compare the ODDs of the auto maker X to the auto maker Y. When trying to purchase a Level 4 AI self-driving car, you might be overwhelmed with having to try and compare the different makes and models.

This might be reminiscent of buying say anti-virus software. You might recall that you used to have to try and compare the different makes and models, as it were, of anti-viral software. They each had a variety of features. It was hard to know which features you really needed or not. The anti-virus software makers would at times add to the confusion by how they described the features. There was no easy way to compare apples-to-apples of one anti-viral software package versus another.

Of course, buying an AI self-driving car is a bit more serious of a task. You are getting something that is a life-critical kind of system. You ought to know when and where it will function.

I'm betting that the marketing of these new-fangled AI self-driving cars will certainly make things more confounding. Rather than trying to get you immersed into the arcane aspects of the set of ODDs, you'll likely instead be shown a slick brochure or video of the AI self-driving car zipping down the highway, not a worry in the world. You will be so wide-eyed that you won't question whether the AI can drive in the snow or in heavy wind conditions.

It is going to be the wild, wild west of ODDs. A potential boondoggle.

You might be wondering how come no one is already taking care of this, prior to it happening.

The biggest reason is that we are still so far away from having Level 4 AI self-driving cars that the matter of the ODDs is just not something the lay public cares about. I've predicted that if the industry won't take care of this on its own, the odds are that once the public gets irked, it could become a matter that draws heavy regulation.

You are likely used to the idea that when you buy a new car there are all sorts of regulated proclamations and declarations that you are legally supposed to receive. There isn't anything as yet about ODDs. If people start to buy Level 4 AI self-driving cars and get upset about being confused or maybe even fooled about the ODDs for a given self-driving car, I'd wager the regulators will jump into the vacuum.

Another reason that the ODD matter hasn't risen to attention is that it is assumed right now that Level 4 AI self-driving cars will be so costly that the average person is not going to be able to afford one. In that case, it is larger firms like ridesharing companies that will be buying the Level 4's. And in that case, presumably those firms will be scrutinizing the ODDs of the fleet of self-driving cars they are amassing.

I have questioned though the idea that only large firms will be buying Level 4 AI self-driving cars. This assumes that the cost of AI self-driving cars will be high, which I generally agree will likely be quite a bit higher than conventional cars. But it also neglects to realize that even the everyday person could potentially afford such a self-driving car if you consider it to be a potential money maker.

If I buy a Level 4 AI self-driving car and put it out for use as a ridesharing car, I can make money doing so. While I am at work, my self-driving car is roaming around and making money. When I am asleep at night, my self-driving car is giving rides and getting money.

This would allow me to afford a "pricey" car because I am offsetting the cost of the car for the revenue that the car can produce for me. Nobody seems to be thinking clearly about how large a cottage industry this will likely create.

Some have suggested that all AI self-driving cars will become commodities. The argument is that they will all ultimately have the same set of features. I've debunked that assertion. It falsely implies that each of the auto makers are going to each duplicate the same kinds of features on their AI self-driving cars. I'd bet that we'll actually have a features war. There will be an ODDs war.

The ODDs war will be that auto maker X says their ODDs are better than auto maker Y. This will go on for quite some time. The usual leap frogging of high-tech and automobiles will of course occur. One year, auto maker X will have a "better" ODD set than auto maker Y. Meanwhile, with continued innovation and advancement, the next year the ODD set of auto maker Y might be better than the ODDs of auto maker X. This will continue, over and over.

Each of the auto makers and tech firms are developing their Level 4 AI self-driving cars in their own proprietary ways. This also means the ODDs are equally as proprietary and idiosyncratic. That's what happens when you don't have any standards in place.

You can anticipate that the ODDs will be somewhat different from each other. There will be overlapping elements. There will be elements that one uses that another does not. There will be elements used by one that another one means something else entirely. If I say that my ODD excludes high winds, but if I don't put something quantifiable and definitive on that condition, you might also say that you exclude high winds, but we are possibly talking about quite different aspects (maybe you mean wind gusts, and I mean the raw average speed of the wind).

It is handy that some researchers are trying to help us out of this mess, doing so before the mess becomes fully evident. For example, Dr. Krzysztof Czarnecki at the University of Waterloo has been putting together a helpful ontology for ODDs. He organizes the proposed ontology into five key areas, consisting of road structure, road users, animals, other obstacles, and environmental conditions. He defines an Operational Road Environmental Model (OREM), consisting of relevant assumptions about the road environment, and then crafts Operational World Models (OWMs) that consist of OREMs with one or more subject vehicle models. This is the kind of rigor we need to get established for ODDs.

If we could get ODDs into a more structured and agreed form and format, it would certainly make the publication and comparison of them a lot easier and more readily understood.

Referring again to the anti-viral software and trying to compare different packages, it seemed like the world eventually settled on a reasonably sensible set of features and it became easier to compare one set versus another. As a buyer, you merely had to inspect a chart and see which features were ticked and included and which were not. I don't though want to mislead into suggesting that the same would be so easily done for Level 4 AI self-driving cars, as the number and variety of the elements of the ODDs is by far much larger and more complex.

I'll toss another idea out there and see what you think of it.

Suppose the auto makers and tech firms were able to compartmentalize their AI systems to correspond to the elements of a defined and standardized ODD. Besides allowing for comparing auto maker X to auto maker Y in terms of their Level 4 AI self-driving cars, we might be able to do something else too.

It might be possible to have auto maker X and auto maker Y offer to do a deal whereby there might elements of each of their respective ODDs that they could exchange with each other. Suppose that one has dealt with handling high winds, while the other one has focused on dealing with snowy conditions. They might opt to share with each other, in which case auto maker X now gets the snowy condition added to its ODD and the auto maker Y gets the high winds condition added to its ODD.

I say this with a grain of salt. A really big grain of salt. The odds are that the hardware and the software of the AI systems of the auto maker X and auto maker Y are so vastly different that it is unlikely they could just offer up their respective components of handling high winds and of snowy conditions to each other. Instead, they each would have something extremely proprietary that works only on their own setup of hardware and AI software.

Imagine though if it was via a magic-wand a possibility to have this kind of interchangeable parts, as it were, for the advent of AI self-driving cars. This suggestion likely causes you to hark back to your history classes. Remember the famous story of Eli Whitney, wherein he built ten guns all containing the same parts and then disassembled them and reassembled them while on the floor of Congress in 1801. He did this to showcase the value of interchangeable parts. Congress subsequently ordered that standards be established.

Could we possibly even have third-party AI developers that then provide add-ons for the ODDs of AI self-driving cars?

It seems farfetched but at least worth postulating. Imagine an entrepreneur that realizes the ODD of the auto maker X lacks a high winds capability and so puts one together and makes it available in some kind of global exchange. If the AI systems have Application Programming Interfaces (APIs) this also provides opportunity for similar kinds of expansion packs.

One quite serious concern would be the aspect that they are cars, which determine the life or death aspects of those that ride in them and also the life or death aspects of those nearby these self-driving cars. Do we want to open up these AI systems to allow for this kind of exchange of parts and expansions? It could produce untoward results. There are also system security issues that need to be considered too.

Conclusion

Will we be able to amalgamate ODD's of Level 4 AI self-driving cars? The jury is still out on this.

Admittedly, it is a stretch right now to think that it could happen. There is too much momentum of each auto maker or tech firm doing their own proprietary ODDs and there is little or no incentive to do otherwise. As I've mentioned, if things get out-of-hand, it could be that regulators step into the morass and offer some kind of sticks and carrots to get ODDs to become more manageable.

I've not said much herein about Level 5 AI self-driving cars.

In theory, a Level 5 AI self-driving car is a complete set of all of the possible ODDs that would exist in a more scattered manner for Level 4 AI self-driving cars. In other words, the Level 5 is not supposed to have any curtailing limits, other than there is no off-roading capability required and also that the driving task must be something that a human driver could have managed (if a human could not have driven in the circumstance, the Level 5 definition says that there should not be an expectation that the AI could).

Some believe that to get to a Level 5, you should first make Level 4 AI self-driving cars. You could then presumably tie together all of the various ODDs over time that you crafted for the Level 4's and make your way to a Level 5. There are those that eschew such an approach and say that you should forget about doing any of the Level 4's. Don't get mired into the itsy-bitsy ODD's. Instead, aim for the whole enchilada. Aim for the Level 5.

If indeed the Level 4's are quickly replaced by Level 5's, it would likely lessen the impact of the ODDs wars and fractionalization. People would barely have had time to complain about the confusion over the myriad of ODDs, and presumably be quieted and more satisfied once they rode in a Level 5. For those that believe we are going to have Level 5's on the heels of Level 4's, the ODD topic is a "don't care" to them. Those ODD's will be like yesterday's fad that came and went. Forget about it, they would assert.

I've said and written many times that a true Level 5 AI self-driving car is like a moonshot.

I hope you can now see why I say this.

The Level 5 has to be able to handle all of the permutations and combinations of all of the ODD's that you can think of.

That's a lot to deal with. I doubt that the time gap between Level 4's and Level 5's is going to be as swift as some pundits claim.

You heard it here first, the role of Operational Design Domains (ODD) is going to be a big topic in the upcoming emergence of AI self-driving cars. Few are talking about it right now.

It is a so-called wonky topic that only AI self-driving car industry insiders know about. Even they don't care much about it, since they are mainly the auto makers and tech firms that are focused on making their own proprietary AI systems for their own proprietary self-driving cars.

I applaud those that are forging a means toward an ontology of ODDs.

We need to do more to get the ODDs matter on-track before it becomes a train that goes off the tracks.

For those that are standing on the railroad tracks right now, it takes a lot of vision to see what's going to happen miles and miles away, into the future.

Imagine if the railroads had not agreed to a common means of laying track, and upon reaching Promontory Summit in Utah on May 10, 1869, they would have not been able to drive that final golden spike into tying together the Central Pacific and the Union Pacific Railroads.

That's the kind of progress that can occur when you get your standards act together.

Let's do the same for ODDs.

.

APPENDIX

APPENDIX A
TEACHING WITH THIS MATERIAL

The material in this book can be readily used either as a supplemental to other content for a class, or it can also be used as a core set of textbook material for a specialized class. Classes where this material is most likely used include any classes at the college or university level that want to augment the class by offering thought provoking and educational essays about AI and self-driving cars.

In particular, here are some aspects for class use:

o   Computer Science. Studying AI, autonomous vehicles, etc.

o   Business. Exploring technology and it adoption for business.

o   Sociology. Sociological views on the adoption and advancement of technology.

Specialized classes at the undergraduate and graduate level can also make use of this material.

For each chapter, consider whether you think the chapter provides material relevant to your course topic. There is plenty of opportunity to get the students thinking about the topic and force them to decide whether they agree or disagree with the points offered and positions taken. I would also encourage you to have the students do additional research beyond the chapter material presented (I provide next some suggested assignments they can do).

RESEARCH ASSIGNMENTS ON THESE TOPICS

Your students can find background material on these topics, doing so in various business and technical publications. I list below the top ranked AI related journals. For business publications, I would suggest the usual culprits such as the Harvard Business Review, Forbes, Fortune, WSJ, and the like.

Here are some suggestions of homework or projects that you could assign to students:

a) <u>Assignment for foundational AI research topic</u>: Research and prepare a paper and a presentation on a specific aspect of Deep AI, Machine Learning, ANN, etc. The paper should cite at least 3 reputable sources. Compare and contrast to what has been stated in this book.

b) <u>Assignment for the Self-Driving Car topic</u>: Research and prepare a paper and Self-Driving Cars. Cite at least 3 reputable sources and analyze the characterizations. Compare and contrast to what has been stated in this book.

c) <u>Assignment for a Business topic</u>: Research and prepare a paper and a presentation on businesses and advanced technology. What is hot, and what is not? Cite at least 3 reputable sources. Compare and contrast to the depictions in this book.

d) <u>Assignment to do a Startup:</u> Have the students prepare a paper about how they might startup a business in this realm. They must submit a sound Business Plan for the startup. They could also be asked to present their Business Plan and so should also have a presentation deck to coincide with it.

You can certainly adjust the aforementioned assignments to fit to your particular needs and the class structure. You'll notice that I ask for 3 reputable cited sources for the paper writing based assignments. I usually steer students toward "reputable" publications, since otherwise they will cite some oddball source that has no credentials other than that they happened to write something and post it onto the Internet. You can define "reputable" in whatever way you prefer, for example some faculty think Wikipedia is not reputable while others believe it is reputable and allow students to cite it.

The reason that I usually ask for at least 3 citations is that if the student only does one or two citations they usually settle on whatever they happened to find the fastest. By requiring three citations, it usually seems to force them to look around, explore, and end-up probably finding five or more, and then whittling it down to 3 that they will actually use.

I have not specified the length of their papers, and leave that to you to tell the students what you prefer. For each of those assignments, you could end-up with a short one to two pager, or you could do a dissertation length paper. Base the length on whatever best fits for your class, and the credit amount of the assignment within the context of the other grading metrics you'll be using for the class.

I mention in the assignments that they are to do a paper and prepare a presentation. I usually try to get students to present their work. This is a good practice for what they will do in the business world. Most of the time, they will be required to prepare an analysis and present it. If you don't have the class time or inclination to have the students present, then you can of course cut out the aspect of them putting together a presentation.

If you want to point students toward highly ranked journals in AI, here's a list of the top journals as reported by *various citation counts sources* (this list changes year to year):

o   Communications of the ACM

o   Artificial Intelligence

o   Cognitive Science

o   IEEE Transactions on Pattern Analysis and Machine Intelligence

o   Foundations and Trends in Machine Learning

o   Journal of Memory and Language

o   Cognitive Psychology

o   Neural Networks

o   IEEE Transactions on Neural Networks and Learning Systems

o   IEEE Intelligent Systems

o   Knowledge-based Systems

GUIDE TO USING THE CHAPTERS

For each of the chapters, I provide next some various ways to use the chapter material. You can assign the tasks as individual homework assignments, or the tasks can be used with team projects for the class. You can easily layout a series of assignments, such as indicating that the students are to do item "a" below for say Chapter 1, then "b" for the next chapter of the book, and so on.

a) What is the main point of the chapter and describe in your own words the significance of the topic,

b) Identify at least two aspects in the chapter that you agree with, and support your concurrence by providing at least one other outside researched item as support; make sure to explain your basis for disagreeing with the aspects,

c) Identify at least two aspects in the chapter that you disagree with, and support your disagreement by providing at least one other outside researched item as support; make sure to explain your basis for disagreeing with the aspects,

d) Find an aspect that was not covered in the chapter, doing so by conducting outside research, and then explain how that aspect ties into the chapter and what significance it brings to the topic,

e) Interview a specialist in industry about the topic of the chapter, collect from them their thoughts and opinions, and readdress the chapter by citing your source and how they compared and contrasted to the material,

f) Interview a relevant academic professor or researcher in a college or university about the topic of the chapter, collect from them their thoughts and opinions, and readdress the chapter by citing your source and how they compared and contrasted to the material,

g) Try to update a chapter by finding out the latest on the topic, and ascertain whether the issue or topic has now been solved or whether it is still being addressed, explain what you come up with.

The above are all ways in which you can get the students of your class involved in considering the material of a given chapter. You could mix things up by having one of those above assignments per each week, covering the chapters over the course of the semester or quarter.

As a reminder, here are the chapters of the book and you can select whichever chapters you find most valued for your particular class:

Chapter Title

Companion Book By This Author

**Advances in AI and Autonomous Vehicles:
Cybernetic Self-Driving Cars**

*Practical Advances in Artificial Intelligence (AI)
and Machine Learning*
by
Dr. Lance B. Eliot, MBA, PhD

This title is available via Amazon and other book sellers

Companion Book By This Author

Self-Driving Cars: "The Mother of All AI Projects"

by Dr. Lance B. Eliot, MBA, PhD

This title is available via Amazon and other book sellers

Companion Book By This Author

Innovation and Thought Leadership on Self-Driving Driverless Cars

by Dr. Lance B. Eliot, MBA, PhD

This title is available via Amazon and other book sellers

Companion Book By This Author

New Advances in AI Autonomous Driverless Cars Self-Driving Cars

by Dr. Lance B. Eliot, MBA, PhD

Chapter Title

This title is available via Amazon and other book sellers

Companion Book By This Author
Introduction to
Driverless Self-Driving Cars

by Dr. Lance B. Eliot, MBA, PhD

This title is available via Amazon and other book sellers

Companion Book By This Author
Autonomous Vehicle Driverless
Self-Driving Cars and Artificial Intelligence
by Dr. Lance B. Eliot, MBA, PhD

This title is available via Amazon and other book sellers

Companion Book By This Author

Transformative Artificial Intelligence
Driverless Self-Driving Cars

by Dr. Lance B. Eliot, MBA, PhD

This title is available via Amazon and other book sellers

Companion Book By This Author

Disruptive Artificial Intelligence and Driverless Self-Driving Cars

by Dr. Lance B. Eliot, MBA, PhD

This title is available via Amazon and other book sellers

Companion Book By This Author

State-of-the-Art
AI Driverless Self-Driving Cars

by Dr. Lance B. Eliot, MBA, PhD

This title is available via Amazon and other book sellers

Companion Book By This Author

Top Trends in
AI Self-Driving Cars

by Dr. Lance B. Eliot, MBA, PhD

This title is available via Amazon and other book sellers

Companion Book By This Author

AI Innovations and Self-Driving Cars

by Dr. Lance B. Eliot, MBA, PhD

<u>Chapter Title</u>

This title is available via Amazon and other book sellers

Companion Book By This Author

Crucial Advances for
AI Self-Driving Cars

by Dr. Lance B. Eliot, MBA, PhD

Chapter Title

This title is available via Amazon and other book sellers

Companion Book By This Author

Sociotechnical Insights and AI Driverless Cars

by Dr. Lance B. Eliot, MBA, PhD

This title is available via Amazon and other book sellers

Companion Book By This Author

Pioneering Advances for AI Driverless Cars

by Dr. Lance B. Eliot, MBA, PhD

This title is available via Amazon and other book sellers

Companion Book By This Author

Leading Edge Trends for AI Driverless Cars

by Dr. Lance B. Eliot, MBA, PhD

This title is available via Amazon and other book sellers

Companion Book By This Author

The Cutting Edge of AI Autonomous Cars

by Dr. Lance B. Eliot, MBA, PhD

This title is available via Amazon and other book sellers

<u>Companion Book By This Author</u>

The Next Wave of
AI Self-Driving Cars

by Dr. Lance B. Eliot, MBA, PhD

<u>Chapter Title</u>

1 Eliot Framework for AI Self-Driving Cars

2 Productivity and AI Self-Driving Cars

3 Blind Pedestrians and AI Self-Driving Cars

4 Fail-Safe AI and AI Self-Driving Cars

5 Anomaly Detection and AI Self-Driving Cars

6 Running Out of Gas and AI Self-Driving Cars

7 Deep Personalization and AI Self-Driving Cars

8 Reframing the Levels of AI Self-Driving Cars

9 Cryptojacking and AI Self-Driving Cars

This title is available via Amazon and other book sellers

Companion Book By This Author

Revolutionary Innovations of
AI Self-Driving Cars

by Dr. Lance B. Eliot, MBA, PhD

Chapter Title

This title is available via Amazon and other book sellers

<u>Companion Book By This Author</u>

AI Self-Driving Cars
Breakthroughs

by Dr. Lance B. Eliot, MBA, PhD

<u>Chapter Title</u>

This title is available via Amazon and other book sellers

Companion Book By This Author

Trailblazing Trends for
AI Self-Driving Cars

by Dr. Lance B. Eliot, MBA, PhD

This title is available via Amazon and other book sellers

<u>Companion Book By This Author</u>

Ingenious Strides for
AI Driverless Cars

by Dr. Lance B. Eliot, MBA, PhD

This title is available via Amazon and other book sellers

This title is available via Amazon and other book sellers

Companion Book By This Author

Visionary Secrets of
AI Driverless Cars

by Dr. Lance B. Eliot, MBA, PhD

This title is available via Amazon and other book sellers

ABOUT THE AUTHOR

Dr. Lance B. Eliot, MBA, PhD is the CEO of Techbruim, Inc. and Executive Director of the Cybernetic AI Self-Driving Car Institute, and has over twenty years of industry experience including serving as a corporate officer in a billion dollar firm and was a partner in a major executive services firm. He is also a serial entrepreneur having founded, ran, and sold several high-tech related businesses. He previously hosted the popular radio show *Technotrends* that was also available on American Airlines flights via their in-flight audio program. Author or co-author of a dozen books and over 400 articles, he has made appearances on CNN, and has been a frequent speaker at industry conferences.

A former professor at the University of Southern California (USC), he founded and led an innovative research lab on Artificial Intelligence in Business. Known as the "AI Insider" his writings on AI advances and trends has been widely read and cited. He also previously served on the faculty of the University of California Los Angeles (UCLA), and was a visiting professor at other major universities. He was elected to the International Board of the Society for Information Management (SIM), a prestigious association of over 3,000 high-tech executives worldwide.

He has performed extensive community service, including serving as Senior Science Adviser to the Vice Chair of the Congressional Committee on Science & Technology. He has served on the Board of the OC Science & Engineering Fair (OCSEF), where he is also has been a Grand Sweepstakes judge, and likewise served as a judge for the Intel International SEF (ISEF). He served as the Vice Chair of the Association for Computing Machinery (ACM) Chapter, a prestigious association of computer scientists. Dr. Eliot has been a shark tank judge for the USC Mark Stevens Center for Innovation on start-up pitch competitions, and served as a mentor for several incubators and accelerators in Silicon Valley and Silicon Beach. He served on several Boards and Committees at USC, including having served on the Marshall Alumni Association (MAA) Board in Southern California.

Dr. Eliot holds a PhD from USC, MBA, and Bachelor's in Computer Science, and earned the CDP, CCP, CSP, CDE, and CISA certifications. Born and raised in Southern California, and having traveled and lived internationally, he enjoys scuba diving, surfing, and sailing.

ADDENDUM

Visionary Secrets of AI Driverless Cars

Practical Advances in Artificial Intelligence (AI) and Machine Learning

By
Dr. Lance B. Eliot, MBA, PhD

———

For supplemental materials of this book, visit:
www.ai-selfdriving-cars.guru

For special orders of this book, contact:
LBE Press Publishing
Email: LBE.Press.Publishing@gmail.com